THE ULTIMATE Insults BOOK

THIS IS A CARLTON BOOK

This edition published 1998 for
Parragon Book Service Ltd
Unit 13–17 Avonbridge Trading Estate,
Atlantic Road, Avonmouth
Bristol BS11 9QD

ISBN 0 75252 736 3

Printed and bound by Firmin-Didot (France)
Group Herissey
N° d'impression : 43646

Author's Acknowledgements:
The author would particularly like to thank Penny Thompson and Crecenzia Jovan Wintergeerst (no, really!) for their invaluable help. Thanks also to Camilla MacWhannell, Julian Flanders and Piers Murray Hill at Carlton Books for all their hard work. This book is dedicated to my old sparring partners, Lawrence Allison, Lucia Forge, Brian Jones and many, many others. I miss you folks! Where are you?

THE ULTIMATE Insults BOOK

Tim Dedopulos

Contents

Misquotation is, in fact, the pride and privilege of the learned. A widely-read man never quotes accurately, for the rather obvious reason that he has read too widely.
Hesketh Pearson, 1887–1972

People are often nasty to each other. Perhaps it's an inevitable result of social contact and free will. Perhaps it fulfils some deep-seated psychological need. Whatever the reason, a lot of folk who really should have known better have been very unpleasant and very funny over the years. This book was written to provide an insight into the whole range of offensive quips and putdowns.

It isn't a modern phenomenon. As you'll see in the first section we have recorded insults from almost 3,000 years ago. William Shakespeare showcases with a section of his own – no other person has done so much to help others express their irritation. His most cutting lines are grouped by play, with short plot synopses for each one. In the next two chapters, you'll see politicians and entertainers respectively with their haloes slipping. After that, it's the turn of national identity. No matter where you come from, someone famous has been very rude about it. The final chapter turns to more common targets.

Most of the lines in this book were spoken by famous people, and recorded in print. Famous people get their comments written down more than the rest of us do. People who are not famous, but who get quoted much, suddenly find that they are famous. You may have seen some of these insults before with different wording, or attributed to different people. Other people use them, they get changed with each repetition, and like Chinese whispers, things mutate. All the insults in here are as accurate and as authentic as I could possibly make them, but if there are any errors, please accept my apologies.

Finally, if you do feel the urge to be really unpleasant to someone, just take a moment to remember how it felt the last time someone put you down cruelly. This book is meant for fun and enlightenment. It's a pretty nasty old world out there, and it can be thoroughly unpleasant without any extra help.

A Brief History of Insults

An injury is much sooner forgotten than an insult.
Lord Chesterfield, 1694–1773

It seems certain that people have been irritated by those around them ever since our first, most distant ancestors spent a night in the same cave. If our closest relatives, the chimps, are anything to go by, we were finding ways to be rude to each other even before we had learnt words to express our displeasure. Love and scorn go hand in hand and disapproval is a basic part of the human psyche. Sometimes, setting diplomacy aside and saying what you truly mean is the only way to get your message across. There are times when you have to be cruel to be kind.

Cynical students of human nature will find it no surprise that the jibes and complaints of ancient cultures are more or less the same as those we have today. The past may be a foreign country, but it is one where the young are as disrespectful and headstrong, the old as foolish and hidebound, the governments as bureaucratic and the powerful as corrupt as they are back home. With apologies to Newton, for every action there is a vocal and opposite detractor. You may be able to fool all of the people some of the time, but you don't have a snowball's chance in hell of pleasing all of the people ever.

Of course, the past is a tricky area to stroll around in. The words of bitter malice that come down to us out of ancient times are those which were recorded in books, plays, articles and speeches. We can only guess at the blood-curdling oaths that flew around the streets of ancient Carthage, and tremble at the thought of the curses that the Babylonians threw at their neighbours. Perhaps that is for the best.

The Classics

In the ancient world, the masters of acid wit – at least, the ones who left the greatest legacy of bile for later generations to pick over – were the Greeks and the Romans. The culture of ancient Greece prized fine literature, rational debate and scientific thought, some of the most fertile breeding grounds for insulting language in existence. Of the acerbic words that have come down to us through history, some of the oldest belong to Homer, author of *The Iliad* and *The Odyssey*, who lived around 850 BC – getting on for 3,000 years ago.

The man who acts the least upbraids the most.
Homer, *c.* 850BC

[He is] the first in banquets but the last in fight.
Homer

Gods! How the son denigrates from the sire.
Homer

Who dares think one thing and another tell, my heart detest him as the Gates of Hell.
Homer

A green old age, unconscious of decay.
Homer

Indeed, a certain wary distrust of their fellows seems to have been characteristic of the Greek temperament, if the following luminaries are anything to go by.

We are all clever enough at envying a famous man while he is yet alive and at praising him when he is dead.
Mimnermus, *c.* 630BC

When a man dies, all his glory among men dies also.
Stesichorus, 630–580BC

One that hath wine as a chain about his wits, such a one lives no life at all.
Alcaeus, 611–580BC

He who mistrusts most should be trusted least.
Theognis, 570–490BC

For whomsoever I do good, they harm me most.
Sappho of Lesbos, *c.* 610BC

Poor Sappho; her complaint is one that has been echoed down the centuries by the unfortunate victims of false friends. She could have made use of the cynical advice in Aesop's fables, which have been instructing and entertaining the young for thousands of years. The stories use satire and foolishness, when needed, to illustrate and comment on human failings, and serve just as well as a reminder to hard-nosed adults:

Any excuse will serve a tyrant.
Aesop, *c.* 550BC, *The Wolf and the Lamb*

It's easy to be brave from a safe distance.
Aesop, *The Wolf and the Kid*

It's not only fine feathers that make fine birds.
Aesop, *The Jay and the Peacock*

Self-conceit may lead to self-destruction.
Ibid.

I will have nought to do with a man who can blow hot and cold with the same breath.
Aesop, *The Man and the Satyr*

Men often applaud an imitation and hiss at the real thing.
Aesop, *The Buffoon and the Countryman*

Never trust the advice of a man in difficulties.
Aesop, *The Fox and the Goat*

In the centuries following Aesop, being more directly unpleasant seems to have come into fashion. The Greeks still furnish the bulk of available unpleasantness, but whether that was a national characteristic or an accident of preserved literature remains unclear. The first contributor below has a clear view on the issue:

Put not thy faith in any Greek.
Euripides, 484–406BC, *Iphigenia in Tauris*

Too lightly opened are a woman's ears.
Aeschylus, 525–456BC, *Ajax*

Lodgings – free from bugs and fleas if possible, if you know of any such.
Aristophanes, 446–380BC, *Frogs*

He collected audiences around him, and flourished and exhibited and harangued.
Ibid.

I have hardly ever known a mathematician who was capable of reasoning.
Plato, 427–347BC, *The Republic*

No human thing is of serious importance.
Ibid.

Of all animals, the boy is the most unmanageable.
Ibid.

Mothers are fonder of their children [than fathers], for they have a more painful share in their production, and they are more certain that they are their own.
Aristotle, 384–322BC, *Nicomachean Ethics*

One more such victory and we are lost.
Pyrrhus, 319–272BC, on beating the Romans at the Battle of Asculum

The ape, the vilest of beasts – how like to us.
Quintus Ennius, 239–169BC

I only wish I may see your head stroked down with a slipper.
Terence, 185–159BC, *Eunuchus*

Demosthenes: The Athenians will kill you, Phocion, if they go crazy.
Phocion: But they will kill you if they come to their senses.
Phocion, *c.* 402–317BC

At the same time as these great thinkers were devoting time to picking holes in their chosen targets, others were lamenting over greater generalities, expressing their scorn, more often than not, for the whole of humanity. In this selection, the Romans join the Greeks with a more or less equal billing.

No one gets rich quickly if he is honest.
Menander, 343–292BC, *The Flatterer*

Marriage, if one will face the truth, is an evil, but a necessary evil.
Menander, unidentified fragment

Immortal Gods! How much does one man excel another! What a difference there is between a wise man and a fool.
Terence, *Eunuchus*

In fine, nothing is said now that has not been said before.
Ibid.

Let them hate, so long as they fear.
Accius, 170–*c.* 86BC, *Atreus*

There is no greater bane to friendship than adulation, fawning and flattery.
Cicero (Marcus Tullius Cicero), 106–43BC, *De Amicitia* XVI

Old age by nature is rather talkative.
Cicero, *De Senectute*

You must look out in Britain that you are not cheated by the Charioteers.
Cicero

I fear the Greeks, even when they bring gifts.
Virgil, 70–19BC, *Aeneid* Book I

This is a fault common to all singers: that among their friends they never are inclined to sing when they are asked; unasked, they never desist.
Horace, 65–8BC, *Satires* Book I

Old men are only walking hospitals.
Horace, *Ars Poetica*

Homer himself has been observed to nod.
Ibid.

As the ancient world began to slip towards the Dark Ages, the Romans stepped forth to take the greasy torch of criticism from the Greeks. The senate of Rome surely echoed throughout its life with the furious insults of angry statesmen, but most of these are lost to us. One of the more acidic orators was Seneca, the dedicated enemy of Carthage; the poet Martial had a decidedly malicious turn of mind, too.

Carthage must be destroyed!
Seneca, 8BC–AD65

We are mad, not only individually but nationally. We check manslaughter and isolated murders, but what of war and the much-vaunted crime of slaughtering whole peoples?
Seneca, *Epistle*

There is no great genius without some touch of madness.
Seneca, *Moral Essays*

What fools these mortals be.
Seneca, *Epistle*

That most knowing person – gossip.
Ibid.

Oh, this age! How tasteless and ill-bred it is.
Catullus, 87–54BC, *Odes*

In comparing various authors with one another, I have discovered that some of the gravest and latest writers have transcribed, word for word, from former works, without making acknowledgement.
Pliny the Elder, 23–79AD, *Natural History*

With man, most of his misfortunes are occasioned by man.
Ibid.

Nothing is more confident than a bad poet
Martial, 40–AD102, *Epigrams* Book I

I could do without your face, Chloe, and without your neck, and your hands, and your limbs, and, to save myself the trouble of mentioning the points in detail, I could do without you altogether.
Martial

Nycilla dyes her locks, 'tis said,
But 'tis a foul aspersion;
She buys them black; they therefore need
No subsequent immersion.
Martial

I know not whether Phoebus fled from the dinner table of Thyestes; at any rate, Ligurinus, we fell from yours. Splendid, indeed, it is, and magnificently supplied with good things; but when you recite you spoil it all. I don't want you to set before me a turbot or a two-pound mullet; I don't want your mushrooms or your oysters. I want you to keep your mouth shut!
Martial

I do not love thee, Doctor Fell,
The reason why I cannot tell;
But this I know, and know full well,

I do not love thee, Doctor Fell.
Martial, as translated by Thomas Brown (1663–1704)

I would that the Roman people had but one neck!
Caligula (Gaius Julius Caesar Germanicus), AD12–41

Old women should not seek to be perfumed
Plutarch, AD46–120, *Lives*

As the Roman Empire grew more decadent and slowly crumbled into chaos, Europe degenerated into barbarism, and the written records of the following millennium are scarce indeed. Those that do remain are, for the greatest part, texts written by monks. While this is very worthy, and preserves a fascinating history, these austere men of the cloth were not, in general, given to spitting malice with their pens. While we must assume that the Dark Ages were filled with people being nasty to each other – and often at swordpoint – the sad fact is that we have little record of it. A few church fathers and other devouts occasionally suffered their venom to record.

Spending time in the theatres produces fornication, intemperance and every kind of impurity.
Saint John Chrysostom, *c.* 345–407

O womb! O belly! O stinking cod, fulfilled of dung and of corruption! At either end of thee, foul is the sound!
Geoffrey Chaucer, 1340–1400

It is not until the sixteenth century that Europe had the leisure and education to once again swap daggers for quills and get back to the business of being unpleasant for posterity. Once it did, however, it burst back with a vengeance in the form of perhaps the greatest literary figure yet known, William Shakespeare. The good bard had a decidedly nasty streak, and his work alone would provide enough material for several encyclopedias of acid wit. He has single-handedly contributed more to the art of creative invective than any other human. As such, it seems only fair to make a quick survey of his plays and pluck the brightest gems of malice from each. You can, of course, skip the summaries and get straight to the offensive bits.

All's Well That Ends Well is the story of a maid – Helena – who heals the King of France and, for her reward, asks for the hand of Lord Bertram in marriage. He consents, then runs off to fight a war in Italy with his habitually deceitful follower Parolles, hoping that death will get him out of it. Hurt, Helena sets out on a pilgrimage and ends in Italy, where she meets Lord Bertram's new lover, Diana. Diana and Helena swap places unknown to Bertram, who sleeps with his betrothed. He later agrees to love Helena and their unborn child. Almost half of the invective below is directed at Parolles.

Little Helen, farewell; if I can remember thee, I will think of thee at court.

The complaints I have heard of you I do not all believe; 'tis my slowness that I do not, for I know you lack not folly to commit them and have ability enough to make such knaveries yours.

You would answer very well to a whipping.

Scurvy, old, filthy, scurvy lord!

Methink'st thou art a general offence, and every man should beat thee. I think thou wast created for men to breathe themselves upon thee.

You are not worth another word, else I'd call you knave.

France is a dog-hole, and it no more merits the tread of a man's foot.

She is too mean to have her name repeated.

He's a most notable coward, an infinite and endless liar, an hourly promise-breaker, the owner of not one good quality.

I spoke with her but once, and found her wondrous cold.

For I knew the young Count to be a dangerous and lascivious boy, who is a whale to virginity, and devours up all the fry it finds.

Drunkenness is his best virtue, for he will be swine-drunk; and in his sleep he does little harm, save to his bedclothes about him.

He hath out-villain'd villainy so far that the rarity redeems him.

He excels his brother for a coward; yet his brother is reputed one of the best that is. In a retreat he outruns any lackey: marry, in coming on he has the cramp.

Use the carp as you may; for he looks like a poor, decayed, ingenious, foolish, rascally knave.

I saw the man to-day, if man he be.

This woman's an easy glove, my lord; she goes off and on at pleasure.

In *Antony and Cleopatra,* Antony – along with Octavius Caesar, son of the ill-fated Julius Caesar – is the co-ruler of the Western world. Antony is married to Fulvia, but living in Egypt with Cleopatra, his lover. Octavius summons Antony back to Rome, and he reluctantly obeys, but only after Fulvia dies of illness. The two men try to patch things up by marrying Antony to Octavia, Octavius's sister. Antony goes back to his old ways though, and Octavius declares war, quickly gaining the upper hand. With the war obviously lost, Antony's best friends, Enobarbus and Eros, both kill themselves, and Antony follows suit. Cleopatra then also commits suicide in grief, by letting asps bite her.

Pray you, stand farther from me.

Thou didst drink the stale of horses and the gilded puddle which beasts would cough at.

Die a beggar.

Experience, manhood, honour, ne'er before did violate so itself.

O slave, of no more trust than love that's hir'd!

Slave, soulless villain, dog! O rarely base!

In their thick breaths, rank of gross diet, shall we be enclouded, and forc'd to drink their vapour.

Duke Frederick is the main villain in *As You Like It,* a comedy. He usurps the position of his older brother, Senior, and banishes him to the forest of Arden, along with Senior's daughter Rosalind. Frederick's daughter

Celia also flees, along with Touchstone the clown, and later Orlando, Rosalind's love, and Adam, Orlando's servant. Orlando's older brother Oliver is sent to find them all. Rosalind and Celia disguise themselves as shepherds – Rosalind pretending to be male – while Orlando and Adam meet up with Senior. Much misunderstanding ensues from the disguises of the two cousins, and Oliver makes up with his younger brother. Eventually, Celia is married to Oliver and Rosalind to Orlando, and Duke Frederick, now converted to the cause of good by a holy man, invites them all back home again.

Her benefits are mightily misplaced.

What shall I call thee when thou art a man?

Like the toad, ugly and venomous.

Sweep on, you fat and greasy citizens.

I think he be transform'd into a beast; for I can nowhere find him like a man.

And in his brain, which is as dry as the remainder biscuit after a voyage, he hath strange places.

Let's meet as little as we can.

I do desire we may be better strangers.

I was seeking for a fool when I found you.

His kisses are Judas's own children.

Certainly, there is no truth in him.

You lisp and wear strange suits.

Men are April when they woo, December when they wed.

Twins are the theme of *The Comedy of Errors.* Egeon and Emelia have twin sons, and twin servants. The family is separated in a storm, and one son and servant grow up in Syracuse with Egeon, the other pair in Ephesus, separate from their mother Emelia, who also lives there. Both sons are called Antipholus; both servants Dromio. Egeon goes to Ephesus looking for his lost son, where he is arrested and sentenced to death for entering enemy territory. The pair from Syracuse also go to Ephesus on business, where everyone confuses them for their twins. After assorted adventures, Egeon is pardoned just before his execution when he recognizes his long-lost Ephesusian son and Emelia returns from the convent with her mightily confused Syracusan son. The latter then starts to pursue his brother's wife's sister for marriage, and they all have a big feast.

There's many a man hath more hair than wit.

If thou art chang'd to aught, 'tis to an ass.
She's the kitchen-wench, and all grease; and I know not what use to put her to but to make a lamp of her and run from her by her own light. I warrant, her rags and the tallow in them will burn a Poland winter. If she lives till doomsday, she'll burn a week longer than the whole world.

[her complexion is] *Swart, like my shoe; but her face nothing like so clean kept; for why, she sweats, a man may go over shoes in the grime of it.*

No longer from head to foot than from hip to hip: she is spherical, like a globe; I could find out countries in her.

He is deformed, crooked, old, and sere, ill-fac'd, worse bodied, shapeless everywhere; vicious, ungentle, foolish, blunt, unkind; stigmatical in making, worse in mind.

Dissembling harlot, thou art false in all.

Coriolanus is a tragedy. The legendary hero Caius Marcius defeats Aufidius, the ruler of the city of Corioli, on behalf of Rome. He is made a representative of the people and named Coriolanus after the town when he returns to Rome. Political rivals fear his power, however, and persuade the people to condemn him to death. He flees, leaving his wife and mother, behind. Coriolanus then finds Aufidius, and plots with him to seize Rome for revenge. Their army ravages the countryside, but Coriolanus's mother persuades him not to attack the city. Coriolanus and Aufidius return to Corioli, now back outside Roman control, where Aufidius murders Coriolanus because of his popularity.

What's the matter, you dissentious rogues that, rubbing the poor itch of your opinion, make yourselves scabs?

He that depends upon your favours swims with fins of lead, and hews down oaks with rushes.

Boils and plagues plaster you o'er, that you may be abhorr'd farther than seen, and one infect another against the wind a mile! You souls of geese that bear the shapes of men.

I find the ass in compound with the major part of your syllables.

Priests must become mockers, if they shall encounter such ridiculous subjects as you.

Your beards deserve not so honourable a grave as to stuff a botcher's cushion or to be entomb'd in an ass's pack-saddle.

More of your conversation would infect my brain.

He's a disease that must be cut away.

You are the musty chaff, and you are smelt above the moon.

The tartness of his face sours ripe grapes; when he walks, he moves like an engine and the ground shrinks before his treading.

Cymbeline is the ageing King of Britain. His two sons were kidnapped 20 years before, leaving only his daughter, Imogen. To ensure the line of succession, Cymbeline orders Imogen to marry her step-brother Cloten; she disobeys, instead marrying Posthumus, a childhood sweetheart. Posthumus is banished from Britain and Imogen is imprisoned. In Rome, Posthumus is mistakenly convinced of Imogen's infidelity, and reacts by sending his servant to kill her. The servant hasn't the heart for it, and instead hides her, where she meets her long-abducted brothers, although she doesn't realize it. Cloten follows, trying to seduce Imogen disguised as Posthumus, but gets his head cut off by one of Imogen's brothers because of his rudeness. Imogen is then poisoned and falls into a death-like sleep. Rome declares war on Britain, and the invading general meets Imogen as she awakes; she joins his army in despair. Cymbeline is captured by the Romans, but freed by his sons. Posthumus is captured by Britons and hauled before Cymbeline and, finally, Imogen returns to her father, the abductor of the sons admits his crime, Imogen and Posthumus are reconciled and allowed to stay married, Rome makes peace, and everyone lives happily ever after.

Away! Thou'rt poison to my blood.

O disloyal thing, that shouldst repair my youth, thou heap'st a year's age on me!

You reek as a sacrifice. Where air comes out, air comes in; there's none abroad so wholesome as that you vent.

Sir, as I told you always, her beauty and her brain go not together.

Thou wrong'st a gentleman who is as far from thy report as thou from honour.

His beastly mind.

A whoreson jackanapes must take me up for swearing, as if I borrowed mine oaths of him.

It is fit I should commit offence to my inferiors.

Caesar's ambition – which swell'd so much that it did almost stretch the sides o' th' world.

Slander, whose edge is sharper than the sword, whose tongue outvenoms all the worms of Nile.

This Cloten was a fool, an empty purse; there was no money in't. Not Hercules could have knock'd out his brains, for he had none.

Hamlet is one of Shakespeare's more popular tragedies. The character of the title is the son of the dead king of Denmark. The hero's uncle, Claudius, takes over as king and marries Gertrude, Hamlet's mother. Hamlet's fears are confirmed when his father's ghost appears and tells how Claudius poisoned him. Fearing for his life, Claudius sends Hamlet to England, but before he leaves he kills his uncle's advisor. Hamlet is kidnapped by pirates in England and ransomed back to Claudius. The advisor's distraught son, Laertes, agrees to duel Hamlet using a poisoned sword at Claudius's request. Claudius also poisons the victory wine, just in case. Gertrude drinks the wine during the fight, Laertes scratches Hamlet, then they accidentally swap swords, and Hamlet also scratches Laertes. Recognizing his coming death, Laertes admits all, Hamlet then stabs Claudius, and, eventually, the principal characters all die, leaving poor Horatio to tell the story.

Frailty, thy name is woman!

As some ungracious pastors do, show me the steep and thorny way to heaven, whiles, like a puff'd and reckless libertine, himself the primrose path of dalliance treads and recks not his own rede.

Something is rotten in the state of Denmark.

So lust, though to a radiant angel link'd, will sate itself in a celestial bed and prey on garbage.

He is open to incontinency.

A foul and pestilent congregation of vapours. What a piece of work is a man!

What should such fellows as I do, crawling between earth and heaven? We are arrant knaves all; believe none of us.

If thou dost marry, I'll give thee this plague for thy dowry: be thou as chaste as ice, as pure as snow, thou shalt not escape calumny.

O, it offends me to the soul to hear a robustious periwig-pated fellow tear a passion to tatters, to very rags.
It out-herods Herod.

Live in the rank sweat of an enseamed bed, stew'd in corruption, honeying and making love over the nasty sty!

My two schoolfellows, Whom I will trust as I will adders fang'd.

At the start of *Henry IV Part 1*, Henry IV is fighting a revolt led by the Welsh and the Earl of Northumberland. Henry is also cross with his son – known as Hal – because of his villainous friends, including fat, corrupt Sir John Falstaff. Henry IV uses a hostage, Mortimer, to force Northumberland's son Hotspur to hand over some Scottish prisoners. Later, Henry IV tells Hal that Hotspur is more worthy of the crown than he; Hal vows to kill Hotspur in battle, and arranges for Falstaff to lead some men in the army. Northumberland falls sick, and Henry IV sends a message to Hotspur offering to pardon the rebels. The message is suppressed by one of Hotspur's allies, and battle is joined. Hal kills Hotspur, Henry IV wins the battle, and Falstaff proves himself a useless coward several times. After executing several of the more odious traitors, Henry IV divides his power with his two sons, Hal and John of Lancaster.

I see a good amendment of life in thee – from praying to purse-taking.

There's neither honesty, manhood, nor good fellowship in thee.

You tread upon my patience.

He made me mad to see him shine so brisk, and smell so sweet, and talk so like a waiting gentlewoman.

We leak in your chimney, and your chamber-lye breeds fleas like a loach.

Peace, ye fat-guts!

There's no more valour in that Poins than in a wild duck.

Falstaff sweats to death and lards the lean earth as he walks along.

Out, you mad-headed ape! A weasel hath not such a deal of spleen as you are toss'd with.

Why, thou clay-brain'd guts, thou knotty-pated fool, thou whoreson obscene greasy tallow-catch.

You starveling, you elf-skin, you dried neat's-tongue, you bull's sizzle, you stockfish – O for breath to utter what is like thee! – you tailor's yard, you sheath, you bowcase, you vile standing tuck!

What a slave art thou to hack thy sword as thou hast done, and then say it was in fight!

Thou art violently carried away from grace. There is a devil haunts thee in the likeness of an old fat man; a tun of man is thy companion. Why dost thou converse with that trunk of humours, that bolting hutch of beastliness, that swoll'n parcel of dropsies, that huge bombard of sack, that stuff'd cloakbag of guts, that roasted Manningtree ox with the pudding in his belly, that reverend vice, that grey iniquity, that father ruffian, that vanity in years?

That villanous abominable misleader of youth, Falstaff, that old white-bearded Satan.

Do thou amend thy face, and I'll amend my life.

Henry IV Part 2 picks up where Part I leaves off. Northumberland's rebellion continues while, in London, Henry IV has tried to separate Hal from Falstaff by sending the rogue with Hal's brother John to fight Northumberland's forces. Hal returns from fighting the Welsh, and finds Henry IV ill. Meanwhile, nagged by his wife and daughter-in-law, Northumberland agrees not to fight personally, and goes into hiding. Coming battle requires that Hal and his companions join John. En route,

Falstaff recruits a group of old friends, commoners, to fight under him. At the battlefield, the rebels learn that Northumberland isn't coming, and offer to disperse in return for amnesty.They are betrayed by John, who arrests them and sends them for execution once their armies are gone. Back in London, Henry IV is heartened by the victory, but still ill he dies. Hal takes the crown as Henry V.

Your means are very slender, and your waste is great.

You are as a candle, the better part burnt out.

Do you set down your name in the scroll of youth, that are written down old with all the characters of age? Have you not a moist eye, a dry hand, a yellow cheek, a white beard, a decreasing leg, an increasing belly? Is not your voice broken, your wind short, your chin double, your wit single, and every part about you blasted with antiquity?

So, thou common dog, didst thou disgorge thy glutton bosom?

He hath eaten me out of house and home; he hath put all my substance into that fat belly of his.

What a disgrace is it to me to remember thy name.

What a maidenly man-at-arms are you become!

A pox damn you, you muddy rascal! Is that all the comfort you give me?

Hang yourself, you muddy conger.

His wit's as thick as Tewksbury mustard.

The fiend hath prick'd down Bardolph irrecoverable; and his face is Lucifer's privy-kitchen, where he doth nothing but roast malt-worms.

Is thy name Mouldy?

Lord, how subject we old men are to this vice of lying!

He was the very genius of famine; yet lecherous as a monkey, and the whores call'd him mandrake.

His passions, like a whale on ground, confound themselves with working.

A ruffian that will swear, drink, dance, revel the night, rob, murder, and commit the oldest sins the newest kind of ways.

Thou damn'd tripe-visag'd rascal.

Thou paper-fac'd villain.

For anything I know, Falstaff shall die of a sweat, unless already he be killed with your hard opinions.

Moving on into *Henry V*, the Church persuades the king to claim sovereignty of France through an ancestor and to fight the French, even offering money to help the war. The Dauphin, the French prince, sends a mocking message, and Henry agrees to attack. Henry uncovers a French plot to have him assassinated by three of his nobles, and has the repentant traitors executed. Henry takes the city of Harfleur, and the French nobles convince the king to fight on. A battle looms and, although dispirited and sickly, Henry's men carry the day. In retaliation, the French defy certain codes and kill all the boys in the unguarded English camp; Henry responds by executing all the French prisoners. On St Crispin's Day, the English massacre the French at the Battle of Agincourt. Henry's forces then meet with the French, and the King of France agrees to let Henry marry his daughter, Katherine, and take control of France.

Put thy face between his sheets, and do the office of a warming-pan.

He'll yield the crow a pudding one of these days.

Thou cruel, ingrateful, savage, and inhuman creature.

Whatsoever cunning fiend it was that wrought upon thee so preposterously hath got the voice in hell for excellence.

A vain, giddy, shallow, humorous youth.

I desire nothing but odds with England.

He hath heard that men of few words are the best men, and therefore he scorns to say his prayers lest he should be thought a coward; but his few bad words are match'd with as few good deeds.

He never broke any man's head but his own, and that was against a post when he was drunk.

Nym and Bardolph are sworn brothers in filching.

Die and be damn'd!

Bardolph, if your Majesty know the man; his face is all bubukles, and whelks, and knobs, and flames o' fire; and his lips blows at his nose, and it is like a coal of fire, sometimes blue and sometimes red; but his nose is executed and his fire's out.

What a wretched and peevish fellow is this King.

That's a perilous shot out of an elder-gun.

I should be angry with you, if the time were convenient.
Wretched slave who, with a body fill'd and vacant mind.

Thou damned and luxurious mountain-goat.

I did never know so full a voice issue from so empty a heart; but the saying is true – the empty vessel makes the greatest sound. Bardolph and Nym had ten times more valour than this roaring Devil.

He be as good a gentleman as the Devil is, as Lucifer and Belzebub himself.

What an arrant, rascally, beggarly, lousy knave.

Here he comes, swelling like a turkey-cock.

If I owe you anything I will pay you in cudgels.

You are a counterfeit cowardly knave.

Henry V dies seven years after the Battle of Agincourt, and in *Henry VI Part 1* there is much trouble brewing. The Dauphin is king in France, and is in revolt, with Lord Talbot taken prisoner and the army weak. At Orléans, the Dauphin loses to the English, but meets a prophetess, Joan la Pucelle (Joan of Arc). Talbot is freed. The French recapture the city, Talbot fighting – and being beaten by – Joan la Pucelle. She marries the Dauphin, then the couple flee as the English recapture the city. Elsewhere, an argument between Richard Plantagenet and Lord Somerset about Richard's father starts the War of the Roses. Richard is made Duke of York by Henry VI, against Somerset's advice. The Dauphin and Joan la Pucelle fight the English and lose, and the French retreat. Talbot goes to Bordeaux to fight the Dauphin, but is outnumbered because Somerset will not provide Richard of York with the horses to send help. Talbot and his son are both killed, and York burns Joan la Pucelle at the stake. In London, Henry VI agrees to a peace settlement, finally settling on marriage to Margaret of Anjou, whom Lord Suffolk hopes to control.

The terror of the French, the scarecrow that affrights our children so.

Your hearts I'll stamp out with my horse's heels and make a quagmire of your mingled brains.

I will chastise this high minded strumpet.

Go forward, and be chok'd with thy ambition!

Thou art a most pernicious usurer; forward by nature, enemy to peace; lascivious, wanton, more than well beseems a man of thy profession and degree.

Vile fiend and shameless courtezan.

Be packing.

O, were mine eye-bans into bullets turn'd, that I in rage might shoot them at your faces!

You, that are polluted with your lusts, stain'd with the guiltless blood of innocents, corrupt and tainted with a thousand vices.

Following straight on from the previous play, *Henry VI Part 2* starts with Suffolk delivering Margaret, having given Anjou and Main back to France.

Gloucester (the king's protector), York and Warwick are upset at the betrayal of England; Cardinal Beaufort of Winchester disagrees. Buckingham, Somerset and Winchester plot to get rid of Gloucester, while Salisbury agrees to help York and Warwick support Gloucester. Winchester and Suffolk have Gloucester's wife arrested for treason as a witch; she is banished. Meanwhile, Henry VI appoints Somerset as French regent. Somerset returns with news that France is lost. Winchester and Suffolk have Gloucester arrested and murdered. Warwick and Salisbury accuse Suffolk of the murder; he is banished, then captured and killed by pirates. York has hired John Cade to start an uprising in Ireland. Cade invades, taking London and killing all the nobles in the city. Henry VI and Margaret flee. Buckingham and Cumberland disperse Cade's army. York arrives from Ireland with troops. He demands that Buckingham kill Somerset, but is refused, so declares his intention to capture the crown. York's sons, Edward IV and Richard III, rally behind him, as do Warwick and Salisbury. Somerset, Cumberland and Buckingham support Henry. At the Battle of St Albans, York kills Cumberland, and the latter's son swears revenge, while Richard III kills Somerset.

Contemptuous base-born callet.

Base dunghill villain and mechanical, I'll have thy head.
Sit there, the lying'st knave in Christendom.

A wonder and a pointing-stock to every idle rascal.

Small curs are not regarded when they grin.

Beaufort's red sparkling eyes blab his heart's malice, and Suffolk's cloudy brow his stormy hate.

Sharp Buckingham unburdens with his tongue the envious load that lies upon his heart.

You put sharp weapons in a madman's hands.

Base slave, thy words are blunt, and so art thou.

Wedded be thou to the hags of hell.

The first thing we do, let's kill all the lawyers.

His breath stinks with eating toasted cheese.

Hence will I drag thee headlong by the heels unto a dunghill, which shall be thy grave, and there cut off thy most ungracious head.

You'll surely sup in hell.

As *Henry VI Part 3* starts, York and Warwick take the throne. When Henry VI enters, York demands the crown. Henry tells him he and his line can have it after Henry dies naturally. York agrees and Henry's allies storm out, Queen Margaret and her son, Prince Edward, joining with the three lords in revolt. Henry decides to try to make up with the queen. Meanwhile, Richard III convinces his father, York, to attack, but the queen arrives with 20,000 men and wins the ensuing battle. York is killed by Cumberland's son, who is then killed in a later battle. Margaret flees to France. Warwick goes there too, to get the king's sister married to Edward IV. They receive news that Edward IV has married Lady Grey; furious and shamed, Warwick pledges to help Margaret, as does King Lewis. Several lords defect to Warwick's forces, including Edward IV's brother, Clarence. Recrowned, Henry VI names Warwick and Clarence protectors of England, and has his nephew, Richmond, taken to Brittany in case it all goes wrong. Henry's forces go to battle Edward IV, and Henry is captured and imprisoned by Edward. Warwick's forces meet Edward's at the Battle of Barnet, and Edward kills Warwick; Clarence goes back to Edward's side. Margaret arrives with reinforcements, but is captured. Her son, Prince Edward, is killed. Finally, Richard III murders Henry VI. Phew! All that, and time for insults too...

O tiger's heart wrapp'd in a woman's hide!

In thy need such comfort come to thee as now I reap at thy too cruel hand!

Go rate thy minions, proud insulting boy.

The common people swarm like summer flies.

He might infect another and make him of the like spirit to himself. If any such be here – as God forbid! – let him depart before we need his help.

Thou misshapen Dick.

Teeth hadst thou in thy head when thou wast born, to signify thou cam'st to bite the world.

Down, down to hell; and say I sent thee thither.

Farewell, sour annoy!

Henry VIII is another historical play. When two of Henry's nobles complain to a third about Cardinal Wolsey, they are swiftly arrested for treason. At court, Queen Katharine tells Henry that Wolsey has levied a tax on the people without his approval. Henry orders Wolsey to revoke it. Wolsey holds a gala; court gossip suggests he is hated by the people, and he is now working against the queen. Wolsey gets one of his minions appointed as Henry's secretary. As Katharine prepares for Henry to divorce her, another noblewoman who has caught Henry's eye, Anne, swears she will not marry the king. At the divorce trial, Katharine sneers at Wolsey and walks out. The king starts to suspect the cardinal of wrong-doing. Wolsey wants Henry to marry the sister of the King of France, while Henry wants to marry Anne. Henry removes Wolsey's power, then marries Anne secretly and gets her pregnant, while both Wolsey and Katharine become ill and die. The play ends with the Archbishop of Canterbury baptizing Henry's new daughter, Elizabeth, and predicting that she will be a great queen.

I can see his pride peep through each part of him.

He begins a new hell in himself.

This butcher's cur is venom-mouth'd.
He, my lady, hath into monstrous habits put the graces that once were his, and is become as black as if besmear'd in hell.

His will is most malignant.

There's mischief in this man.

Your heart is cramm'd with arrogancy, spleen, and pride.

I abhor this dilatory sloth.

You have as little honesty as honour.

All goodness is poison to thy stomach.

He was a man of an unbounded stomach.

You are strangely troublesome.

Bless me, what a fry of fornication is at door!

Three times was his nose discharged against me; he stands there like a mortar-piece, to blow us.

The tale of *Julius Caesar* is a tragedy rather than a history, and it predates events in *Antony and Cleopatra.* After defeating Pompey, the Roman Senate plans to make Caesar king, but this is opposed by a senator named Cassius, who plans to kill him. Various bleak omens seem to back Cassius up. Various other senators are swayed by Cassius's arguments, fearing Caesar's power if crowned. Caesar ignores many warnings to stay home on the fateful day, and is murdered in the Senate. His friend Antony whips the commoners into a riot in retaliation, and the plotters flee. Antony takes control of Rome with Caesar's son Octavius and Lepidus, while Cassius and his fellows raise an army against them. Antony's forces eventually win, and the plotters, in the main, commit suicide.

You blocks, you stones, you worse than senseless things!

O you hard hearts, you cruel men.

He is a dreamer; let us leave him.

The rabblement hooted and clapped their chopped hands and threw up their sweaty nightcaps and uttered such a deal of stinking breath.

What rubbish, and what offal.

Where wilt thou find a cavern dark enough to mask thy monstrous visage?

Your purpled hands do reek and smoke.

You show'd your teeth like apes, and fawn'd like hounds, and bow'd like bondmen.

I do find it cowardly and vile.

King John ascends the throne after the death of his brother, Richard I, but he is opposed by Richard's legitimate son Arthur, and also by Richard's bastard son, Philip. The various claimants end up in France, seeking help from the king and/or to stop the king helping the other side. The French king clashes with John, and they fight; the peace treaty includes a cessation of hostility, effectively strengthening John on the throne. However, John is excommunicated by the Pope, and the King of France reneges on the peace agreement so as to avoid trouble. In the following battles, John captures Arthur and sends him back to England to be killed and the Pope persuades the French prince, the Dauphin, to claim the English throne too. The English lords, upset about Arthur, go over to the Dauphin's side. John repents to the Pope, being let back into the church. The lords discover that the Dauphin plans to kill them and switch back to John's side, and the English forces beat the French. As John lies dying of poison – administered by a monk – his own son, Henry, appears and he is named as the new king.

On my knee I give heaven thanks I was not like to thee!

He hath a half-face.

If his name be George, I'll call him Peter.

What cracker is this same that deafs our ears with this abundance of superfluous breath?

So vile a lout.

That same purpose-changer, that sly devil, that broker that still breaks the pate of faith, that daily break-vow.

This bawd, this broker, this all-changing word.

Grim, ugly, and sland'rous to thy mother's womb, full of unpleasing blots and sightless stains, lame, foolish, crooked, swart, prodigious, patch'd with foul moles and eye-offending marks.

What a fool art thou, a ramping fool, to brag and stamp and swear.

Thou cold-blooded slave.

Thou odoriferous stench! sound rottenness!

Thy detestable bones.

Out, dunghill!

Thou art more deep damn'd than Prince Lucifer.

There is not yet so ugly a fiend of hell as thou shalt be.

The tragedy of *King Lear* is a tale of foolish pride and betrayal. In old age, Lear retires and divides up his power between his three daughters. The youngest, Cordelia, refuses to flatter him, and gets nothing, while the other two, Goneril and Regan, win marriage to powerful dukes and get Lear's authority divided between them. The King of France, impressed by Cordelia, marries her. Lear becomes offended by his elder daughters' behaviour towards him, and as they and their husbands start a war against him he stomps off out into a storm. Cordelia and the French are called in to help Lear, who is going insane. A loyal noble, Gloucester, hides Lear from the rebels, trying to keep him from capture and death. Goneril is planning to murder her husband and marry Gloucester's bastard son Edmund. Regan, widowed, also wants to marry him. Lear and the French meet up, but both Lear and Cordelia are captured in battle by Edmund, who sends them to be killed. Goneril kills Regan and herself in jealousy over Edmund, and the latter is himself mortally wounded in a fight. Edmund confesses all the evil he has stirred up throughout the play, and then Lear arrives with the dead Cordelia and dies grieving over her death.

An admirable evasion of whore-master man, to lay his goatish disposition to the charge of a star!

I have seen drunkards do more than this in sport.

A knave; a rascal; an eater of broken meats; a base, proud, shallow, beggarly, three-suited, hundred-pound, filthy, worsted-stocking knave; a lily-liver'd, action-taking, whoreson, glass-gazing, superserviceable, finical rogue; one-trunk-inheriting slave; one that wouldst be a bawd in way of good service, and art nothing but the composition of a knave, beggar, coward, pander, and the son and heir of a mongrel bitch.

What a brazen-fac'd varlet art thou.

You whoreson cullionly barbermonger!

Thou whoreson zed! thou unnecessary letter!

Thou art a boil, a plague sore, an embossed carbuncle in my corrupted blood.

False of heart, light of ear, bloody of hand; hog in sloth, fox in stealth, wolf in greediness, dog in madness, lion in prey.

This is the foul fiend Flibbertigibbet.

Poor Tom, that eats the swimming frog, the toad, the todpole, the wall-newt and the water; that in the fury of his heart, when the foul fiend rages, eats cow-dung for sallets, swallows the old rat and the ditch-dog.

Thou art a traitor; false to thy gods, thy brother, and thy father.

From th' extremest upward of thy head to the descent and dust beneath thy foot, a most toad-spotted traitor.

A change of pace from the histories and tragedies, *Love's Labour Lost* is a poetic comedy. King Ferdinand of Spain imposes severe conditions on the young men who study at his court, including that they must never see, speak to or be with a woman. When the daughter of the King of France comes to Ferdinand's court demanding repayment of a disputed debt, she brings several ladies with her. The students predictably become interested in the ladies, sending various letters that get muddled up and misdirected, and Ferdinand himself is interested in the French princess. All fall in love, and decide to set their oaths aside. There then follows a costumed performance where everyone is disguised and the men get confused over the women, before identities are restored and the ladies agree to marry the men if they will complete a year in pilgrimages.

The music of his own vain tongue doth ravish like enchanting harmony.

A whitely wanton with a velvet brow, with two pitch balls stuck in her face for eyes.

Pernicious and indubitate beggar.

You talk greasily; your lips grow foul.

A most pathetical nit!

His intellect is not replenished; he is only an animal, only sensible in the duller parts.

He that is likest to a hogshead.

Ah, you whoreson loggerhead, you were born to do me shame.

Thou halfpenny purse of wit, thou pigeon-egg of discretion.

He hath been five thousand year a boy.

A huge translation of hypocrisy, vilely compil'd, profound simplicity.

Weed this wormwood from your fruitful brain.

Known as "the Scottish Play" because its very name is held to bring bad luck, *Macbeth* is a tale of witchcraft and murder. Already Thane of Glamis, Macbeth meets three witches after a battle, who predict that he will become Thane of Cawdor and then king afterwards. Duncan, the current King of Scotland, rewards Macbeth's valour in the battle by making him Thane of Cawdor, which makes him think about the crown. Lady Macbeth persuades her husband to murder the king and frame his son, Malcolm – the current Prince Regent – for the deed, which duly happens. Macbeth is crowned, despite having gone a bit mad during the event, presumably from pressure. Macbeth has others killed to increase his security, and sees various ghosts and phantasmal illusions. He visits the witches again to seek reassurance, and hears predictions that seem to confirm his safety, but the prophecies are fulfilled by Malcolm's returning forces. Lady Macbeth kills herself, and Macbeth himself is slain in battle, with the crown returning to the rightful heir.

You should be women, and yet your beards forbid me to interpret that you are so.

Whose horrid image doth unfix my hair and make my seated heart knock at my ribs.

In swinish sleep their drenched natures lie.

Destroy your sight with a new Gorgon.

Where we are there's daggers in men's smiles.

You secret, black, and midnight hags.

You egg! Young fry of treachery!

Fit to govern? No, not to live.

A dwarfish thief.

All that is within him does condemn itself for being there.

It is a tale told by an idiot, full of sound and fury, signifying nothing.

In *Measure For Measure*, Duke Vincentio leaves Vienna in the control of a deputy, Angelo, although he assumes various disguises and stays in Vienna. The Duke wants immorality and brothels cleared out of Vienna, and for Angelo to receive the public's hatred for this. Claudio, a young gentleman of the city, is sentenced to death for getting his fiancée pregnant. Various people plead for mercy from Angelo, who offers to grant it if Claudio's sister Isabella, a nun, will sleep with him – she refuses, even to save her brother's life, since she is devout. The Duke, disguised as a friar, hatches a plan to appease Angelo by reuniting him with his lost love, Mariana. The latter will disguise herself as Isabella and sleep with Angelo. The death warrant on Claudio is not lifted, however, and the Duke, still disguised, arranges to have someone else's head presented to Angelo as proof of Claudio's death. The Duke then pretends to return to the city, and hears Isabella's story, along with testament from Mariana and a genuine friar. He marries Angelo to Mariana, sentences Angelo to death, relents, and finally brings Claudio out from jail and releases him.

Thy bones are hollow; impiety has made a feast of thee.

Come, you are a tedious fool. To the purpose.

Your bum is the greatest thing about you; so that, in the beastliest sense, you are Pompey the Great.

O you beast! O faithless coward! O dishonest wretch! Wilt thou be made a man out of my vice?

I'll pray a thousand prayers for thy death.

Thy sin's not accidental, but a trade.

It is certain that when he makes water his urine is congeal'd ice.

Silence that fellow. I would he had some cause to prattle for himself.

Away with those giglets.

A fool, a coward, one all of luxury, an ass, a madman!

Antonio is *The Merchant of Venice.* His friend, Bassanio, want to marry Portia, and needs money to pursue her. Antonio agrees to provide security for a loan from Shylock, an enemy of Antonio's. Portia must marry the suitor who passes a specific test; two suitors fail, then Bassanio – whom Portia loves – makes the correct choice. Antonio is relying on one of his boats returning within three months so that he can repay Shylock, but the boat is wrecked and, in the time it takes Bassanio to travel back to Venice from Portia's house to repay the loan, Shylock declares default on Antonio and has him arrested. Portia disguises herself as a doctor of law and travels to Venice too, with her maid. At the court, Shylock is demanding his contractual right to cut a pound of flesh from Antonio's chest and cannot be dissuaded, although Bassanio has offered him twice as much money as he originally borrowed. Portia turns the contract back on Shylock, showing that he is conspiring to kill Antonio. Antonio is duly freed from the contract, Shylock loses half his possessions, and everyone else lives happily ever after.

There are a sort of men whose visages do cream and mantle like a standing pond.

Gratiano speaks an infinite deal of nothing.

His reasons are as two grains of wheat hid in two bushels of chaff: you shall seek all day ere you find them, and when you have them they are not worth the search.

I had rather be married to a death's-head with a bone in his mouth.

When he is best, he is a little worse than a man, and when he is worst, he is little better than a beast.

A villain with a smiling cheek, a goodly apple rotten at the heart.

O, these deliberate fools!

A bankrupt, a prodigal, who dare scarce show his head on the Rialto.

Soft and dull-ey'd fool.

A stony adversary, an inhuman wretch, uncapable of pity, void and empty from any dram of mercy.

Thy currish spirit govern'd a wolf who, hang'd for human slaughter, even from the gallows did his fell soul fleet, and, whilst thou layest in thy unhallowed dam, infus'd itself in thee; for thy desires are wolfish, bloody, starv'd and ravenous.

Beg that thou mayst have leave to hang thyself.

Sir John Falstaff, the rogue from *Henry IV*, is at the centre of *The Merry Wives of Windsor*. Falstaff is seeking marriage to Anne Page. Also seeking Anne's affections are Slender, the local judge's cousin, Caius, a French doctor, and Fenton, a young gentleman. Falstaff plans to seduce and steal money from two of the wives of the village, Mrs Ford and Mrs Page, Anne's mother. Offended at the idea, his associates reveal Falstaff's plan to the ladies and their husbands. The ladies plan a revenge, and string Falstaff along through a variety of comic encounters, playing him for all the fool he's worth. Meanwhile, Slender, Caius and Fenton continue to vie for Anne's hand. Mr Page favours Slender, while Mrs Page favours Caius. Anne, of course, favours Fenton. The two couples plan a final joke on Falstaff, with the ladies arranging to meet him by an old oak tree, where he will be bedevilled by various folk dressed up as fairies. While this happens, Anne slips off and marries Fenton, and Falstaff learns that he has been the butt of a huge joke all along.

You Banbury cheese!

How now, Mephostophilus!

I say the gentleman had drunk himself out of his five sentences.

O base Hungarian wight!

Rogues, hence, avaunt! vanish like hailstones, go.

What tempest, I trow, threw this whale, with so many tuns of oil in his belly, ashore at Windsor?

The wicked fire of lust have melted him in his own grease.

I will find you twenty lascivious turtles ere one chaste man.

Ford's a knave, and I will aggravate his style.

I will rather trust a Fleming with my butter, Parson Hugh the Welshman with my cheese, an Irishman with my aqua-vitae bottle, or a thief to walk my ambling gelding, than my wife with herself.

King-Urinal.

This unwholesome humidity, this gross wat'ry pumpion; we'll teach him to know turtles from jays.

I had rather be set quick i' th' earth and bowl'd to death with turnips.

Art thou lunatics?

Dishonest varlet! we cannot misuse him enough.

Out of my door, you witch, you hag, you baggage, you polecat, you ronyon!

The devil will not have me damn'd, lest the oil that's in me should set hell on fire.

Vile worm, thou wast o'erlook'd even in thy birth.

She's a great lubberly boy.

In *A Midsummer Night's Dream*, the Duke of Athens, Theseus, decrees that Hermia must marry Demetrius, although she loves Lysander. Helena, Hermia's friend, loves Demetrius, and when she hears that Hermia and Lysander are running away into the forest she tells Demetrius. Meanwhile, in the forest, Oberon, King of the Fairies, obtains a love-charm to use on his wife Titania as part of a ploy to get a servant boy from her. At the same time, he sends Puck to sort out the tangled lovers by using the charm to make Demetrius love Helena. Circumstances conspire against the ploy; first Lysander is made to love Helena, and then Demetrius is too. To solve the problems, Oberon magics up a fog to separate the four and send them to sleep, so the charm can wear off. He then makes up with Titania. The four humans are woken by Theseus. Lysander tells of his love for Hermia and Demetrius of his re-awakened love for Helena, and they are allowed to marry as they will.

Ill met by moonlight.

Rash wanton.

You hard-hearted adamant.

Tempt not too much the hatred of my spirit; for I am sick when I do look on thee.

I do repent the tedious minutes I with her have spent.

What hempen homespuns have we swagg'ring here?

If you were men, as men you are in show, you would not use a gentle lady so.

Have you no modesty, no maiden shame, no touch of bashfulness?

Get you gone, you dwarf; you minimus, of hind'ring knot-grass made; you bead, you acorn.

This is the silliest stuff that ever I heard.

A charming comedy following the tangled skein of two very different romances, *Much Ado About Nothing* centres on the reluctant relationship between Benedick and Beatrice, two sharp-witted enemies of marriage, and on the burgeoning love between Claudio and Hero. While Benedick and Beatrice trade insults, Claudio enlists the help of the prince, Don Pedro, to woo Hero. After various confusions of identity stirred by John, Pedro's malicious bastard brother, Pedro unites Claudio and Hero. Hero, Claudio, Pedro and others then conspire to make Beatrice and Benedick marry. Meanwhile, John uses trickery to make Hero appear a whore; Claudio denounces her at her wedding, and she pretends death from the shock. Benedick and Beatrice admit their love to each other. Benedick challenges Claudio to a duel, but before they can fight John's lies are uncovered. Hero's father, who knows she's still alive, tells Claudio that as compensation for Hero's "death", he shall marry a "cousin" of hers the next day. The next morning all is revealed, Claudio is consoled and re-engaged to Hero, Benedick and Beatrice also become engaged, and John is arrested.

Four of his five wits went halting off, and now is the whole man govern'd with one.

If he have wit enough to keep himself warm, let him bear it for a difference between himself and his horse.

I do not like thy look, I promise thee.

Men from children nothing differ.

Boys, apes, braggarts, jacks, milksops!

Scambling, outfacing, fashion-monging boys, that lie and cog and flout, deprave and slander, go anticly, show outward hideousness, and speak off half a dozen dang'rous words, how they might hurt their enemies, if they durst; and this is all.

Art thou the slave that with thy breath hast kill'd?

You have such a February face, so full of frost, of storm, and cloudiness.

The tragedy of *Othello* is based in Venice. Iago seeks revenge against Othello for choosing Cassio as lieutenant. Iago manages to fool Cassio into disgracing himself, then convinces him to ask Othello's wife, Desdemona, to help persuade Othello to reinstate him. Iago then starts hinting to Othello about an affair between Desdemona and Cassio, even planting evidence. Othello, enraged, names Iago lieutenant and tells him to kill Cassio. Iago persuades Othello to murder Desdemona that night, while he kills Cassio. The same day a letter arrives summoning Othello from Cyprus back to Venice, and appointing Cassio in his place for the duration. Iago arranges for Cassio to be killed by a fellow conspirator who desires Desdemona, but Cassio survives and Iago kills the wounded conspirator to keep him silent. Othello then kills Desdemona. When the truth comes out shortly after Desdemona's death, Othello commits suicide and Cassio takes Iago to torture and kill.

You rise to play, and go to bed to work.

A slippery and subtle knave.

An index and obscure prologue to the history of lust and foul thoughts.

O curse of marriage, that we can call these delicate creatures ours, and not their appetites!

I had rather be a toad, and live upon the vapor of a dungeon, than keep a corner in the thing I love for others' uses.

Damn her, lewd minx!

You are welcome, sir, to Cyprus. Goats and monkeys!

This is a subtle whore, a closet lock and key of villainous secrets.

Heaven truly knows that thou art false as hell.

She's like a liar gone to burning hell.

She was a whore.

I think upon't, I think, I smell't, O villainy!

O, she was foul!

Pericles, Prince of Tyre goes to Tharsus to avoid the wrath of a Syrian king. He relieves a famine there, then gets word that a Syrian is coming there to kill him. He flees again, but is shipwrecked, ending up in Pentapolis, where he falls for and marries Thaisa, daughter of King Simonides. He then hears that the Syrian king is dead and heads home. Thaisa dies en route giving birth to a daughter, Marina, and is buried at sea in a casket. For her safety, Pericles leaves Marina at Tharsus, returning to Tyre. Thaisa's corpse is found meanwhile, and she is restored to life by magic; she takes religious vows. Years pass and Marina is captured by pirates in Tharsus – saving her from murder by her jealous guardians – and sold to a brothel where she becomes a music teacher, not a whore. When Pericles visits the city she lives in, the governor unknowningly reunites them. The goddess Diana then tells Pericles to visit Ephesus; when he does, he finds his long-lost wife. The governor marries Marina and they go to rule Tyre, and Pericles and Thaisa take over in Pentapolis where Simonides has recently died.

Courtesy would seem to cover sin.

Both like serpents are, who, though they feed on sweetest flowers, yet they poison breed.

What a drunken knave the sea was to cast thee in our way!

Thou art the rudeliest welcome to this world.

He did not flow from honourable sources.

Thou art like the harpy, which, to betray, dost with thine angel's face, seize with thine eagle's talons.

The pox upon her green-sickness.

Your peevish chastity is not worth a breakfast in the cheapest country.

Thy food is such as hath been belch'd on by infected lungs.

The first of the sequence of historical plays chronicling the life of Henry IV is *Richard II*. At its beginning Henry Bolingbroke (who will later become Henry IV) is banished from England for five years. His father dies, and King Richard II seizes his lands. Several nobles, unhappy with the king – including the Earl of Northumberland and his son Hotspur – help Bolingbroke back to England. York, Bolingbroke's uncle, does not approve. Bolingbroke defeats and executes several nobles against whom he has grievances and, with the help of York's armies, forces Richard to hand over the crown, becoming Henry IV. Richard is imprisoned and York's son – Henry IV's cousin – plots to poison Henry. The king finds out and, although he pardons his cousin, several other nobles are executed. Richard is murdered in prison.

God and good men hate so foul a liar.

It issues from the rancour of a villain, a recreant and most degenerate traitor.

Now put it, God, in the physician's mind to help him to his grave immediately!

Pray God we may make haste, and come too late!

Snakes, in my heart-blood warm'd, that sting my heart! Three Judases, each one thrice worse than Judas!

Thou little better thing than earth.

Thou haught insulting man.

Fiend, thou torments me ere I come to hell.

Go thou and fill another room in hell.

Richard III marks the end of the sequence of plays detailing the War of the Roses. Richard has convinced the sickly Edward IV to jail their brother, Clarence, then has him murdered. Edward IV dies and Richard imprisons

Queen Elizabeth's sons with the help of Buckingham, and puts Edward IV's sons in the Tower of London. Richard then has Elizabeth's brother and one of her sons killed. Richard takes the throne and Elizabeth sends her last son, Dorset, to see Richmond, Henry VI's nephew. Richard marries Anne, Henry VI's widowed daughter-in-law, then has the princes in the tower killed, and also his own wife and Clarence's son Edward. Richmond raises an army with the help of Buckingham and others and invades. Richard executes Buckingham, then has a horrific dream where his victims all return to curse him. The same ghosts visit Richmond and encourage him. The armies meet at Bosworth Field, where Richmond kills Richard. He is then crowned Henry VII and marries Richard's niece, reuniting the houses of York and Lancaster.

Not shap'd for sportive tricks, nor made to court an amorous looking-glass.

Curtail'd of this fair proportion, cheated of feature by dissembling nature, deform'd, unfinish'd.

Thou lump of foul deformity.
'Tis thy presence that exhales this blood from cold and empty veins where no blood dwells.

Thou unfit for any place but hell.

Never hung poison on a fouler toad.

Out of my sight! Thou dost infect mine eyes.

Thou elvish-mark'd, abortive, rooting hog, thou that wast seal'd in thy nativity the slave of nature and the son of hell, thou slander of thy heavy mother's womb, thou loathed issue of thy father's loins, thou rag of honour.

Poisonous bunch-back'd toad.

Deep, hollow, treacherous, and full of guile.

A knot you are of damned blood-suckers.

Thy mother's name is ominous to children.

Wretched, bloody, and usurping boar.

Perhaps the most famous Shakespeare play of all, *Romeo and Juliet* is set in Verona. The two are from feuding families, and meet when Romeo, depressed over his unrequited love for Rosaline, attends a party held by Juliet's father. The two fall in love, despairing when they hear they are from enemy families. Romeo persuades a sympathetic priest to marry them, which he does that afternoon. Juliet's cousin tries to fight Romeo and ends up killing a friend of his; Romeo slays him in revenge, and is banished from the city. Juliet's father arranges a marriage to a suitor he favours. To stop Juliet killing herself in despair, the priest provides her with a potion which will fake death for two days, giving her time to be laid to rest, and arranges to tell Romeo, so that they can flee together. The priest's message goes astray and Romeo hears of Juliet's "death", so goes to her tomb, fights and kills her suitor, then kills himself in Juliet's tomb. Juliet awakes, finds Romeo dead and also kills herself. When the two families find out the truth of the matter, their feud is put aside and they swear to build statues to remember the two lovers.

Why he's a man of wax.

When good manners shall lie all in one or two men's hands, and they unwash'd too, 'tis a foul thing.

You kiss by th' book.
He heareth not, he stirreth not, he moveth not; the ape is dead.

She speaks, yet she says nothing.

The very butcher of a silk button.

These strange flies, these fashion-mongers.

What saucy merchant was this that was so full of his ropery?

He is not the flower of courtesy.

Thy head is as full of quarrels as an egg is full of meat.

You ratcatcher.

A dog, a rat, a mouse, a cat, to scratch a man to death!

A plague o' both your houses!

O serpent heart, hid with a flow'ring face!

Despised substance of divinest show!

A wretched puling fool, a whining mammet.

Hang, beg, starve, die in the streets.
Thou detestable maw, thou womb of death.

An early comedy, *The Taming of the Shrew* concerns the daughters of a Paduan gentleman. Several men are pursuing the hand of the sweet Bianca, but her father has decreed that none may pursue her while her bad-tempered sister, Katherina, remains unmarried. Two of the suitors, Lucentio and Hortensio, manage to fool the father into accepting them as tutors to

Bianca and both attempt to use this opportunity to pay court to her.A friend of Hortensio's, Petruchio, hearing that Kate has a large dowry on account of her objectionability, goes to the house.After sparring with Kate verbally, he is doubly convinced and asks for her hand, getting it immediately. While various layers of deception surround the suitors for Bianca, Petruchio whisks Kate off and subjects her to many unpleasant ordeals in order to beat obedience into her, which he does, nearly brainwashing her. Hortensio gives in and marries a widow he's long liked, while Lucentio marries Bianca in secret and, after some anger on both fathers' parts, all celebrate.

How foul and loathsome is thine image!

Think'st thou, Hortensio, though her father be very rich, any man is so very a fool to be married to hell?

There's small choice in rotten apples.

I know she is an irksome brawling scold.

Lead apes in hell.

If I be waspish, best beware my sting.

He was a frantic fool, hiding his bitter jests in blunt behaviour.

A monster, a very monster in apparel.

Away, you three-inch fool!

You heedless joltheads and unmanner'd slaves!
Am I your bird? I mean to shift my bush.

When she is forward, peevish, sullen, sour, and not obedient to his honest will, what is she but a foul contending rebel and graceless traitor?

Some 12 years before the start of *The Tempest,* Prospero – the Duke of Milan – was overthrown by his brother, Antonio, with help from Alonso, King of Naples, and abandoned at sea with his daughter, Miranda. When the play begins, Alonso and Antonio are on a ship which is caught in a storm caused by Prospero, courtesy of his sorcerous powers. They are magically brought to Prospero's island, and think themselves marooned. Miranda meets Alonso's son, Ferdinand, and they fall in love. Prospero watches the various nobles and servants in plot and counter-plot against each other and himself, foiling all their plans sorcerously. Finally, he reveals himself, gives Miranda to Ferdinand and forgives his enemies. Alonso in turn restores Prospero's dukedom.

His complexion is perfect gallows.

Hang, cur; hang, you whoreson, insolent noisemaker.

Hell is empty, and all the devils are here.

Toads, beetles, bats, light on you!

Thou most lying slave.

Hag-seed, hence!

Look, he's winding up the watch of his wit; by and by it will strike.

What strange fish hath made his meal on thee?
All the infections that the sun sucks up from bogs, fens, flats, on Prospero fall, and make him by inch-meal a disease!

What have we here? a man or a fish? dead or alive?

Bite him to death, I prithee.

O, ho, monster.

Most wicked sir, whom to call brother would even infect my mouth.

The theme of the satirical play *Timon of Athens* is that of money. Timon is far too generous. His steward, Flavius, fears mounting debt. Others have noticed, and various senators to whom Timon owes money suddenly panic and all demand immediate repayment. Timon turns to his friends – those he has been so generous to – for help and all refuse him. In the end, to avoid execution, he flees into the woods and lives as a hermit, quickly coming to hate mankind. He finds a cache of buried gold left for him by the gods and gives much of it to a passing Athenian captain, Alcibiades, who argued for mercy for Timon and is now attacking Athens. Flavius also gets a gift. Passing rumours of his horde, Timon attracts his old false friends out to see him and leads each one along for a while before chasing them off. Finally, Timon dies and Alcibiades holds the city to ransom, extorts payment from Timon's false friends and tells all to remember the man.

That there should be small love amongst these sweet knaves, and all this courtesy! The strain of man's bred out into baboon and monkey.

He's opposite to humanity.

I wonder men dare trust themselves with men.

Those healths will make thee and thy state look ill.
They were the most needless creatures living.

Hoy-day, what a sweep of vanity comes this way!

We may account thee a whoremaster and a knave.

Thou disease of a friend.

You breathe in vain.

His days are foul and his drink dangerous.

Live loath'd and long, most smiling, smooth, detested parasites, courteous destroyers, affable wolves.

There's nothing level in our cursed natures but direct villainy. Therefore be abhorr'd all feasts, societies, and throngs of men!

I do wish thou wert a dog, that I might love thee something.

Thy lips rot off!

Be a whore still; they love thee not that use thee. Give them diseases.

Were I like thee, I'd throw away myself.

When there is nothing living but thee, thou shalt be welcome.

I had rather be a beggar's dog.

Would thou wert clean enough to spit upon!

I'll beat thee – but I should infect my hands.

Away, thou issue of a mangy dog! Choler does kill me that thou art alive.

Live, and love thy misery!

A particularly gory play, the tragedy of *Titus Andronicus* is set in Rome. Saturninus, the new emperor, marries Titus's daughter, Lavinia, although she is in love with his brother. The lovers run off together and Saturninus declares he prefers Tamora – a captured Goth queen – and marries her. Tamora's sons both also desire Lavinia, so at the suggestion of Tamora's lover, Aaron, they murder her lover, rape her and sever her tongue and hands. Tamora and Aaron frame two of Titus's sons for the murder of Lavinia's lover, and they are duly killed. Lavinia manages to convey what happened. Tamora gives birth to Aaron's child; Aaron kills the nurse and midwife to try to cover it up and hides the baby. Titus's remaining son attacks Rome with the help of the Goths, having captured Aaron. In exchange for the baby's life, Aaron confesses all the carnage and torture he has caused. Back in Rome, Titus kills Tamora's sons and serves them to Tamora and Saturninus as pies. While they eat, Titus kills Lavinia to end her suffering, explains what happened to her to Saturninus, and reveals what the two have just eaten. He then kills Tamora, Saturninus kills him, and Lucius kills Saturninus and is proclaimed emperor. Tamora's corpse is thrown to the birds, while Aaron is buried up to his chest and starved to death.

Thou dost over-ween in all.

Foul-spoken coward, that thund'rest with thy tongue, and with thy weapon nothing dar'st perform.

What a caterwauling dost thou keep!

As loathsome as a toad.

Say, wall-ey'd slave, whither wouldst thou convey this growing image of thy fiend-like face?

O most insatiate and luxurious woman!

The Greeks are waging war on Troy to reclaim a kidnapped queen, Helen, in *Troilus and Cressida.* Troilus is a Trojan prince, in love with Cressida. Hector, another prince, is inclined to return Helen, and his sister, Cassandra, predicts doom if he does not, but their brothers Troilus and Paris – who Helen is now happily married to – persuade him not to. Cressida's uncle plays matchmaker, bringing her together with Troilus in love. In the Greek camp, Cressida's traitorous father, who has converted to the Greek side, asks that the Greeks exchange a prisoner for Cressida. The exchange goes ahead and Diomedes, a Greek, starts pursuing Cressida. Following a challenge between Hector and his Greek cousin Ajax, Troilus spies on Cressida and finds that she is unfaithful. At a battle the next day, Troilus kills many but cannot avenge himself on Diomedes, while Hector, his brother, is killed by Achilles. The play then ends with Cressida's uncle cursing himself and Troy seemingly doomed.

He is melancholy without cause.

A slave whose gall coins slanders like a mint.

Why, this hath not a finger's dignity.

I would thou didst itch from head to foot and I had the scratching of thee; I would make thee the loathsomest scab in Greece.
Thou stool for a witch!

Thou sodden-witted lord!

Thou hast no more brain than I have in mine elbows.

Thou thing of no bowels, thou!

Though you bite so sharp at reasons, you are so empty of them.

That were to enlard his fat-already pride.

A paltry, insolent fellow!

I had rather be a tick in a sheep than such a valiant ignorance.

Her wanton spirits look out at every joint and motive of her body.

Set them down for sluttish spoils of opportunity, and daughters of the game.

Thou core of envy!

Thou crusty batch of nature.

Why, thou full dish of fool.

Thou damnable box of envy.

You ruinous butt; you whoreson indistinguishable cur.

Thou idle immaterial skein of sleid silk, thou green sarcenet flap for a sore eye, thou tassel of a prodigal's purse, thou.
He has not so much brain as ear-wax.

Nothing but lechery! All incontinent varlets!

Bastard begot, bastard instructed, bastard in mind, bastard in valour, in everything illegitimate.

Twelfth Night is another comedy of mistaken twins. Viola and Sebastian are shipwrecked and separated, each fearing the other drowned. Viola disguises herself as a man and becomes the servant of Duke Orsino. The Duke sends her to woo a rich countess, Olivia, on his behalf. Olivia, however, falls in love with Viola, thinking she is a man. Viola herself is keen on the Duke. Viola is challenged to a duel by another suitor of Olivia's, but the fight is broken up by a friend of Sebastian's, Antonio, who has arrived with him in the town. Antonio is then arrested, as the Duke is an enemy of his. Meanwhile, Sebastian gets into a duel which is broken up by Olivia. She thinks he is Viola, who she still thinks is male, and declares her love; Sebastian loves her at first sight and they get married. Following confusion where Olivia calls a shocked Viola her husband, everything is sorted out and the Duke vows to marry Viola.

A fellow o' th' strangest mind i' th' world.

Go to, y'are a dry fool; I'll no more of you.

He speaks nothing but madman.

Lady, you are the cruell'st she alive.

What a caterwauling do you keep here!

Observe him, for the love of mockery.
I do care for something; but in my conscience, sir, I do not care for you. If that be to care for nothing, sir, I would it would make you invisible.

You are now sail'd into the north of my lady's opinion; where you will hang like an icicle on Dutchman's beard

I can hardly forbear hurling things at him.

A fiend like thee might bear my soul to hell.

Fie, thou dishonest Satan!

Leave thy vain bibble-babble.

An ass-head and a coxcomb and a knave, a thin fac'd knave, a gull.

Proteus and Valentine, *The Two Gentlemen of Verona*, are good friends. They separately travel to Milan, Proteus leaving his love, Julia, behind. In Milan, Valentine and Silvia, the Duke's daughter, are in love, although the Duke favours a match to the foolish Thurio. When Proteus arrives, he too immediately desires Silvia. Proteus betrays Valentine's plan to elope with Silvia. Proteus tries to woo Silvia, but she is put off by his perfidy, spurring Proteus to greater heights. Julia, who has come to Milan in disguise, discovers Proteus's love for Silvia, and is devastated. Silvia tell the disguised Julia that she will have nothing to do with Proteus because of his cruelty to Julia. Silvia runs away and is captured by bandits; even when rescued by Proteus, she will not love him. Valentine saves her when Proteus threatens force, but he then forgives Proteus. When Julia removes her disguise, Proteus vows to be true to her. The Duke then blesses the union between Valentine and Silvia.

You, minion, are too saucy.

If you spend word for word with me, I shall make your wit bankrupt.
She is peevish, sullen, forward, proud, disobedient, stubborn, lacking duty.

She hath more hair than wit, and more faults than hairs, and more wealth than faults.

She is lumpish, heavy, melancholy.

Degenerate and base art thou.

Finally, in *The Winter's Tale*, the King of Sicily, Leontes, wrongly comes to suspect his wife Hermione of being unfaithful with the King of Bohemia, his boyhood friend Polixenes. Lord Camillo helps Polixenes flee the city unmolested, defecting to the Bohemian court. Leontes puts Hermione in prison, where she bears his child. Believing the baby to belong to Polixenes, Leontes orders it abandoned, and the baby girl is left in the forests of Bohemia. An oracle tells Leontes he is completely wrong. He repents, but is told that Hermione is dead from grief and, accepting blame, he swears to visit her tomb every day. Sixteen years pass and the abandoned girl, Perdita, is now being courted by Polixenes's son Florizel. His father forbids a match to a commoner, but Camillo, wanting to return to Sicily, helps the lovers flee there. They are chased to Sicily by Polixenes, and a box of Perdita's in his possession proves that she is Leontes's daughter. The two kings rejoice and bless the match, then Hermione comes out of hiding and goes back to her husband.

Should all despair that hath revolted wives, the tenth of mankind would hang themselves.

My wife's a hobby-horse.

I hate thee; pronounce thee a gross lout, a mindless slave.
Go rot!

She is spread of late into a goodly bulk.

We need no grave to bury honesty; there's not a grain of it the face to sweeten of the whole dungy earth.

Thou hast need of more rags to lay on thee.

Having flown over many knavish professions, he settled only in rogue.

If you had but look'd big and spit at him, he'd have run.

Thou fresh piece of excellent witchcraft.

You are rough and hairy.

His garments are rich, but he wears them not handsomely.

Here come those I have done good to against my will.

Although he is still immensely popular and one of the cornerstones of the English language, Shakespeare is by no means universally adored. You may find that you are distinctly unimpressed. If so, you are in noble company. Several of the great and the good have taken a swipe, suggesting in the most intemperate terms that as far as they are concerned, the man is not the genius that other people believe.

When I read Shakespeare I am struck with wonder
That such trivial people should muse and thunder
In such lovely language.
D.H. Lawrence, 1885–1930, *When I Read Shakespeare*

And Hamlet – how boring, how boring –
To live with so mean and self-conscious,
Blowing and snoring.
Ibid.

The players have often mentioned it as an honour to Shakespeare that, in his writing, whatsoever he penned, he never blotted out a line. My answer hath been, "Would that he had blotted a thousand".
Ben Johnson, 1573–1637, *Timber*

I am more easily bored with Shakespeare and have suffered more ghastly evenings with Shakespeare than with any other dramatist I know.
Peter Brook, 1925–

It would positively be a relief to dig him up and throw stones at him.
George Bernard Shaw, 1856–1950

Throughout the sixteenth, seventeenth and eighteenth centuries, there was a gradual picking up of the arts offensive in European and American literature. Many people reflected rather rudely on the human condition – a long-standing habit of ours if ever there was one.

Man, in sooth, is a marvellous, vain, fickle and unstable subject.
Michel de Montaigne, 1533–1592, *Essays*

Sits he ever so high on a throne, a man still sits on his bottom.
Ibid.

Thou little thinkest what foolery governs the world.
John Selden, 1584–1654, *Table Talk*

Few men make themselves masters of the things they think and write.
Ibid.

Besides us and my Uncle Fenner's family, there was none of any quality but poor and rascally people.
Samuel Pepys, 1633–1703, *Diary*

Men are generally more careful of the breed of their horses and dogs than of their children.
William Penn, 1644–1718, *Fruite of Solitude*

That vain, ill-natured thing, an Englishman.
Daniel Defoe, 1661–1731, *The True Born Englishman*

Despite the prejudices of medieval Europe, it would never do for women to feel left out. Even back then, there was plenty of ill-feeling to go around.

If women were by nature what they make themselves by artifice, if their faces suddenly became so bright or so leaden as they make themselves by paint, they would be inconsolable.
Jean de la Bruyère, 1645–1696, *Les Caratères*

Tho' marriage makes man and wife one flesh, it leaves them still two fools.
William Congreve, 1670–1729, *The Double Dealer*

Every woman who is not absolutely ugly thinks herself beautiful.
Philip Stanhope, Earl of Chesterfield, 1694–1773, *Letters*

Sir, a woman preaching is like a dog walking on its hind legs. It is not done well; but you are surprised to find it done at all.
Samuel Johnson, 1709–1784

Other writers chose more specific targets, taking particular offence at certain subsections of the world – the educated, the uneducated, the religious, the sacrilegious; in fact, almost anything that the writer was not.
Much reading is an oppression of the mind, and extinguishes the natural candle; which is the reason of so many senseless scholars in the world.
William Penn, *Advise to his Children*

Of all the plagues with which mankind are curst, ecclesiastical tyrrany's the worst.
Daniel Defoe, *The True Born Englishman*

Let blockheads read what blockheads write.
Philip Stanhope, Earl of Chesterfield, 1694–1773, *Letters*

This agglomeration which was called, and which still calls itself, the Holy Roman Empire is neither Holy, nor Roman, nor an Empire.
Voltaire, 1694–1778, *Essai sur les Moeurs*

Public schools are the nurseries of all vice and immorality.
Henry Fielding, 1707–1754, *Joseph Andrews*

The newspapers! Sir, they are the most villainous, licentious, abominable, infernal – not that I ever read them.
R.B. Sheridan, 1751–1816, *The Critic*

Our ancestors are very good kind of folks, but they are the last people I should choose to have a visiting acquaintance with.
R.B. Sheridan, *The Rivals*

There is not in the Universe a more ridiculous nor a more contemptible animal than a proud clergyman.
Henry Fielding, *Amelia*

Although in general the years leading up to the nineteenth century were fairly restrained in terms of directly personal criticism – at least, whatever remains available to study today – one luminary does stand out as a viperish, ill-tempered and thoroughly entertaining character. Samuel Johnson was a critic, poet and biographer, and he was the compiler of the first English dictionary. He was also completely comfortable speaking his mind.

Tom Birch is as brisk as a bee in conversation; but no sooner does he take a pen to his hand than it becomes a torpedo to him and benumbs all his faculties.
Samuel Johnson, 1709–1784

The noblest prospect which a Scotchman ever sees is the high road that leads him to England.
Samuel Johnson

Much may be made of a Scotchman – if he be caught young.
Samuel Johnson

Sherry is dull, naturally dull; but it must have taken him a great deal of pains to become what we see him now. Such an excess of stupidity, sir, is not in nature.
Samuel Johnson, on Thomas Sheridan

That was a good enough dinner to be sure, but it was not a dinner to ask a man to.
Samuel Johnson

He is one of the many who have made themselves public without making themselves known.
Samuel Johnson, on William Kenrick

The fellow seems to me to possess but one idea, and that is a wrong one.
Samuel Johnson

No man was more foolish when he had not a pen in his hand.
Samuel Johnson, on Dr Goldsmith

An honest politician is one who, when he is bought, will stay bought.
Simon Cameron, 1799–1889

Politics is a unique field. While most of us are cynical about the intentions and beliefs of our leaders, we are still prone to violent disagreements with people of opposing political views. We look down on people who subscribe to the other side, despite the fact that we ourselves often do not particularly believe in the position that we are holding or in the honesty of the politicians we support. Dogma and rhetoric do not fit in particularly well with the real world; life is built on practicalities, and it doesn't make much difference who you voted for when the washing machine has just flooded the kitchen. Politicians argue and thunder at each other – and provide a lot of highly amusing insults in the process, as we shall see – but even they do not seem to believe themselves, let alone each other.

Since a politician never believes what he says, he is quite surprised to be taken at his word.
Charles de Gaulle, 1890–1970

Persistence in one opinion has never been considered a merit in political leaders.
Cicero, 106–43BC, *Ad Familiares*

Politicians are the same all over. They promise to build a bridge even where there is no river.
Nikita Khruschev, 1894–1971

The left is a group of people who will never be happy unless they can convince themselves that they are about to be betrayed by their leaders.
Richard Crossman, 1907–1974, *Diary*

A gentleman will blithely do in politics what he would kick a man downstairs for doing in ordinary life.
Earl Rosebery, 1847–1929

He knows nothing and thinks he knows everything. That points clearly to a political career.
George Bernard Shaw, 1856–1950, *Major Barbara*

A good politician is quite as unthinkable as an honest burglar.
H.L. Mencken, 1880–1956, *Minority Report*

Politics and the fate of mankind are shaped by men without ideals and without greatness. Men who have greatness within them don't go in for politics.
Albert Camus, 1913–1960, *Notebooks*

The authorities were at their wits' end, nor had it taken them long to get there.
Desmond McCarthy, 1877–1952

Indeed, it is not just disbelief that politicians seem to associate with their chosen field, and they are most certainly not alone in feeling critical of the system. People from all walks of public life view government with a cynical eye and a jaundiced opinion.

Mein Kampf *is really the most honest book any politician has ever written.*
W.H. Auden, 1907–1973

The trouble with this country is that there are too many politicians who believe, with a conviction based of experience, that you can fool all of the people all of the time.
Franklin Adams, 1881–1960, *Nods and Becks,* on gullibility

When the political columnists say "Every thinking man", they mean themselves; when the candidates appeal to "every intelligent voter", they mean everybody who intends to vote for them.
Franklin Adams

Congress... these – for the most part – illiterate hacks whose fancy vests are spotted with gravy and whose speeches, hypocritical, unctuous and slovenly, are spotted also with the gravy of political patronage.
Mary McCarthy, 1912–, *On The Contrary*

A politician is an arse upon which everyone has sat except a man.
E.E. Cummings, 1894–1962, *One Times One*

The presidency is now a cross between a popularity contest and a high school debate, with an encyclopaedia of clichés as first prize.
Saul Bellow, 1915–

A horrible voice, bad breath, and a vulgar manner – the characteristics of a popular politician.
Aristophanes, *c.* 440–380BC

Politics and religion have always had fairly strong ties – sometimes mutually cooperative, sometimes antagonistic, depending on whether the State and the Church were competing for influence with the people, or cooperating over it. Given this somewhat ambivalent relationship throughout history, it is perhaps unsurprising that some of the sternest (and rudest) critics of religion have come from the ranks of politicians and political commentators. Among the most verbal of religion's critics have been the political philosophers Friedrich Nietzsche and Thomas Paine.

Parasitism is the only practice of the church, with its ideal of anaemia, its "holiness", draining all blood, all love, all hope for life; the beyond as the will to negate every reality; the cross as the mark of recognition for the most subterranean conspiracy that ever existed – against health, beauty, whatever has turned out well, courage, spirit, graciousness of the soul, against life itself. I call Christianity the one great curse, the one great innermost corruption, the one great instinct of revenge, for which no means is poisonous, stealthy, subterranean, small enough – I call it the one immortal blemish of mankind.
Friedrich Nietzsche, 1844–1900, *The Antichrist*

Whatever a theologian regards as true must be false; there you have almost a criterion of truth.
Friedrich Nietzsche

Whenever we read the obscene stories, the voluptuous debaucheries, the cruel and torturous executions, the unrelenting vindictiveness, with which more than half the Bible is filled, it would be more consistent that we called it the word of a demon than the Word of God. It is a history of wickedness that has served to corrupt and brutalize mankind, and for my own part, I sincerely detest it, as I detest everything that is cruel.
Thomas Paine, 1737–1809, *The Age of Reason*, on the Bible

It appears to me as a species of atheism – a sort of religious denial of God. It professes to believe in man rather than in God. It is as near to atheism as twilight to darkness. It introduces between man and his Maker an opaque body, which it calls a Redeemer, as the moon introduces her opaque self between the earth and the sun, and it produces by this means a religious or irreligious eclipse of the light. It has put the whole orbit of reason into shade.
Thomas Paine, on Christian faith

What is it the New Testament teaches us? To believe that the Almighty committed debauchery with a woman engaged to be married; and the belief of this debauchery is called faith.
Ibid., on comparative morality

All religions, with their gods, demigods, prophets, messiahs and saints, are the product of the fancy and credulity of men who have not yet reached the full development and complete possession of their intellectual powers.
Mikhail Bakunin, 1814–1876, *Dieu et l'état*

Theologians are all alike, of whatever religion or country they may be; their aim is always to wield despotic authority over men's consciences; they therefore persecute all of us who have the temerity to tell the truth.
Frederick the Great, 1712–1786, private correspondence

Other commentators took it all a bit less seriously, preferring to poke gentler fun.

Many a long dispute between divines may be thus abridged: It is so. It is not so. It is so. It is not so.
Benjamin Franklin, 1706–1790, *Poor Richard's Almanack*

A cult is a religion with no political power.
Tom Wolfe, 1931–, *In Our Time*

People who feel themselves to be exiles in this world are mightily inclined to believe themselves citizens of another.
George Santayana, 1863–1952

Why do born-again people so often make you wish they'd never been born the first time?
Katherine Whitehorn, 1926–, in the *Observer* newspaper

Theology – an effort to explain the unknowable by putting it into the terms of the not worth knowing.
H.L. Mencken, 1880–1956, *Senentiae*

We must respect the other fellow's religion, but only in the sense and to the extend that we respect his theory that his wife is beautiful and his children smart.
H.L. Mencken, *Minority Report*

Faith may be defined briefly as an illogical belief in the occurrence of the improbable.
H.L. Mencken

The chief contribution of Protestantism to human thought is its massive proof that God is a bore.
HL Mencken

Several important political figures commented on the popularity of religion, in frustration, sadness or gleeful avarice, depending on their personal philosophies.

Religion is the idol of the mob; it adores everything it does not understand.
Frederick the Great, 1712–1786, private correspondence

Religion is excellent stuff for keeping the common people quiet.
Napoleon Bonaparte, 1769–1821

Religion is the sign of the oppressed creature, the feeling of a heartless world and the spirit of conditions which are unspiritual. It is the opium of the people.
Karl Marx, 1818–1883

Regardless of this cynicism, few politicians and commentators, however, have been as persistently dubious about both politics and humanity at large as the Irish-born Whig politician, Edmund Burke. Strongly critical of the French Revolution, he still thought Parliament should not attempt to coerce the American settlers, and believed in the freedom of Ireland. Many Conservatives regard him as their greatest political thinker – although there are those who disagree.

I am not one of those who think that the people are never in the wrong. They have been so, frequently and outrageously, both in other countries and in this. But I do say that in all disputes between them and their rulers, the presumption is at least upon a par in favour of the people.
Edmund Burke, 1729–1797, *Thoughts on the Cause of the Present Discontent*

I have in general no very exalted opinion of the virtue of paper government.
Edmund Burke, *On Conciliation With America*

To tax and to please, no more than to love and be wise, is not given to men.
Edmund Burke, *On American Taxation*

Men will not look to acts of parliament, to regulations, to declarations, to votes and resolutions. No, they are not such fools. They will ask, what is the road to power, credit, wealth and honours? They will ask, what conduct ends in neglect, disgrace, poverty, exile, prison and gibbet? These will teach them the course which they are to follow. It is your distribution of these that will give the character and tone to your government. All the rest is miserable grimace.
Edmund Burke

Where two motives, neither of them perfectly justifiable, may be assigned, the worst has the chance of being preferred.
Edmund Burke

History consists, for the greater part, of the miseries brought upon the world by pride, ambition, avarice, revenge, lust, sedition, hypocrisy, ungoverned zeal,

and all the train of disorderly appetites.
Edmund Burke, *Reflections on the Revolution in France*

By hating vices too much, they come to love men too little.
Ibid.

This sort of people are so taken up with their theories about the rights of man that they have totally forgotten his nature.
Ibid.

The age of chivalry is gone – that of sophisters, economists and calculators has succeeded; and the glory of Europe is extinguished for ever.
Ibid.

Because half a dozen grasshoppers under a fern make the field ring with their importunate chink, whilst thousands of great cattle, reposed beneath the shadow of the British oak, chew the cud and are silent, pray do not imagine that those who make the noise are the only inhabitants of the field.
Ibid.

It is a general popular error to imagine the loudest complainers for the public to be the most anxious for its welfare.
Edmund Burke, *Observations in a late Publication on the Present State of the Nation*

Burke was a damned wrong-headed fellow, through his whole life jealous and obstinate.
Charles James Fox, 1749–1806, on Edmund Burke

As he rose like a rocket, so he fell like a stick.
Thomas Paine, 1737–1809, on Edmund Burke

Oft have I wondered that on Irish ground
No poisonous reptiles ever yet were found;
Reveals the secret strands of nature's work,
She sav'd her venom to create a Burke.
Warren Hastings, 1732–1818, on Edmund Burke

While politicians may or may not all be the same, there are some definite local variations. One of the most notable is that British politicians seem to be considerably more rude to each other than their counterparts in other countries. Other governments have plenty of insulting members of course but, in terms of the sheer volume of nasty jibes and sarcastic sniping that comes out of Westminster's Houses of Parliament, Britain leads the world. Furthermore, one particularly waspish voice stands out from the general babble of British politics – that of Sir Winston Churchill. He was one of the most dominant members of the British political scene for much of the twentieth century, despite spending a lot of that time being marginalized for his views. He was a powerful, emphatic man who looked a bit like a bulldog and a bit like a newborn baby, depending on your point of view. He was also extremely sharp-witted and had a tongue to match. The majority of his scorn was reserved for his political opponents.

He is one of those orators of whom it was well said, "Before they get up, they do not know what they are going to say; when they are speaking, they do not know what they are saying; and when they have sat down, they do not know what they have said."
Winston Churchill, 1874–1965, on Lord Charles Beresford

I remember, when I was a child, being taken to the celebrated Barnum's Circus, which contained an exhibition of freaks and monstrosities; but the exhibit on the programme which I most desired to see was the one described as "The Boneless Wonder". My parents judged that the spectacle would be too

demoralizing and revolting for my youthful eyes, and I have waited fifty years, to see The Boneless Wonder sitting on the Treasury Bench.
Winston Churchill, on Ramsay MacDonald

A curious mixture of geniality and venom.
Winston Churchill, on Herbert Morrison

Mr Gladstone read Homer for fun, which I thought served him right.
Winston Churchill, on Gladstone

The happy warrior of Squandermania.
Winston Churchill, on Lloyd George

Unless the right honourable gentleman changes his policy and methods and moves without the slightest delay, he will be as great a curse to this country in peace as he was a squalid nuisance in time of war.
Winston Churchill, on Aneurin Bevin

They are not fit to manage a whelk-stall.
Winston Churchill, on the British Labour Party

There he stalks, that Wuthering Height.
Winston Churchill, on John Reith

He was particularly scornful of Clement Attlee, a mild, unassuming man – for a politician, anyway; Sir Stafford Cripps, an ascetically minded and deeply religious politician; and Stanley Baldwin, the Conservative leader who failed to prepare Britain for the Second World War.

A sheep in sheep's clothing.
Winston Churchill, on Clement Attlee

A modest man who has much to be modest about.
Winston Churchill, on Clement Attlee

An empty taxi arrived at 10 Downing Street, and when the door was opened, Attlee got out.
Winston Churchill, on Clement Attlee, although Churchill denied the attribution

He delivers his speech with an expression of injured guilt.
Winston Churchill, on Stafford Cripps

There but for the grace of God, goes God.
Winston Churchill, on Stafford Cripps

I wish Stanley Baldwin no ill, but it would have been much better if he had never lived.
Winston Churchill, on Stanley Baldwin

The candle in that great turnip has gone out.
Winston Churchill, on Stanley Baldwin's later years.

He occasionally stumbled over the truth, but hastily picked himself up and hurried on as if nothing had happened.
Winston Churchill, on Stanley Baldwin

Another target were the Chamberlain family. The father, Joseph, had been a minister for both Conservative and Liberal governments. One of his sons, Austen, was famed for his advocacy of the League of Nations, while the other, Neville, became known as the Man of Munich.

Mr Chamberlain loves the working man; he loves to see him work.
Winston Churchill on Joseph Chamberlain

He always played the game, and he always lost it.
Winston Churchill, on Austen Chamberlain

He looked at foreign affairs through the wrong end of a municipal drainpipe.
Winston Churchill, on Neville Chamberlain

In the depths of that dusty soul there is nothing but abject surrender.
Winston Churchill, on Neville Chamberlain

The utmost he has been able to gain for Czechoslovakia and in the matters which were in dispute is that the German dictator, instead of snatching his victuals from the table, has been content to have them served to him course by course.
Winston Churchill, on Neville Chamberlain

An appeaser is one who feeds a crocodile hoping it will eat him last.
Winston Churchill, on Neville Chamberlain

Churchill was also more than happy to be offensive to his female colleagues, if the opportunity presented itself.

Lady Astor, to Churchill: *"Winston, if you were my husband, I should flavour your coffee with poison."*
Churchill: *"Madam, if I were your husband, I should drink it."*

Bessie Braddock, to Churchill: *"Winston, you're drunk!"*
Churchill: *"Bessie, you're ugly. And tomorrow morning, I shall be sober."*

Although known for his sallies in the House of Commons, Churchill was hardly any more tolerant outside of Parliament. Generals, playwrights and even whole countries felt his bite.

The greatest cross I have to bear is the cross of Lorraine.
Winston Churchill on Charles de Gaulle

In defeat unbeatable; in victory unbearable.
Winston Churchill, on General Montgomery

What could you hope to achieve except to be sunk in a bigger and more expensive ship this time?
Winston Churchill, to Admiral Mountbatten, in response to the latter's protests at being given a desk job in 1941.

Naval tradition? Monstrous. Nothing but rum, sodomy, prayers, and the lash.
Winston Churchill

A riddle wrapped in a mystery inside an engima.
Winston Churchill, on Russia

It becomes still more difficult to reconcile Japanese action with prudence or even with sanity.
Winston Churchill, on Japan

When George Bernard Shaw invited Churchill to the first performance of a new play, he enclosed two tickets, saying *"Bring a friend – if you have one"*. Churchill politely declined: *"I cannot come. Would it be possible for you to let me have tickets for the second night – if there is one?"*

Throughout his life, Churchill also displayed a fair amount of scorn for the entire field of politics. His disdain for his colleagues individually was matched only by his scorn for them collectively.

I am never going to have anything more to do with politics or politicians. When this war is over, I shall confine myself entirely to writing and painting.
Winston Churchill, to a fellow First World War officer at the front during 1915.

It would be a great reform in politics if wisdom could be made to spread as easily and as rapidly as folly.
Winston Churchill

No-one pretends that democracy is perfect or all-wise. Indeed, it has been said that democracy is the worst form of Government except all those other forms that have been tried from time to time.
Winston Churchill

When I am abroad, I always make it a rule never to criticize or attack the Government of my country. I make up for lost time when I am at home.
Winston Churchill

Cultured people are merely the glittering scum which floats upon the deep river of production.
Winston Churchill, to his son Randolph

It would be a mistake to imagine that Sir Winston had everything his own way, though. There were plenty of detractors and political opponents waiting to take a swipe – particularly Aneurin Bevan, the Labour politician. Even Attlee sometimes stooped to take a pop.

Fifty percent of Winston is genius, fifty percent bloody fool. He will behave like a child.
Clement Attlee, 1883–1967, on Winston Churchill

I must remind the right honourable gentleman that a monologue is not a decision.
Clement Attlee, to Winston Churchill

He never spares himself in conversation. He gives himself so generously that hardly anybody else is permitted to give anything in his presence.
Aneurin Bevan, 1897–1960, on Winston Churchill

I welcome this opportunity of pricking the bloated bladder of lies with the poinard of truth.
Aneurin Bevan, to Winston Churchill

The Tories always hold the view that the state is an apparatus for the protection of the swag of the property owners… Christ drove the money-changers out of the temple, but you inscribe their title deed on the altar cloth.
Aneurin Bevan, to Winston Churchill

The Prime Minister has got very many virtues, and when the time comes I hope to pay my tribute to them, but I am bound to say that political honesty and sagacity have never been among them.
Aneurin Bevan, on Winston Churchill

He is a man suffering from petrified adolescence.
Aneurin Bevan, on Winston Churchill

He is not a man for whom I ever had esteem. Always in the wrong, always surrounded by crooks, a most unsuccessful father – simply a "radio personality" who outlived his prime.
Evelyn Waugh, 1903–1966, on Winston Churchill

Bevan was noted for his acerbic wit and frequently displayed a wide streak of malice – even when he wasn't talking about Churchill. The son of a Welsh miner, he himself became a miner at the age of 13, which undoubtedly proved good training for entering politics. A dedicated socialist, he founded the British National Health Service, and became the deputy leader of the Labour Party in 1959, the year before his death. Like his old foe Winston, he was scathing about several colleagues, including Chamberlain.

The worst thing I can say about democracy is that it has tolerated the right honourable gentleman for four and a half years.
Aneurin Bevan, 1897–1960, on Neville Chamberlain

Listening to a speech by Chamberlain is like paying a visit to Woolworth's: everything in its place and nothing above sixpence.
Aneurin Bevan

He seems determined to make a trumpet sound like a tin whistle... He brings to the fierce struggle of politics the tepid enthusiasm of a lazy summer afternoon at a cricket match.
Aneurin Bevan, on Clement Attlee

No amount of cajolery, and no attempts at ethical or social seduction, can eradicate from my heart a deep burning hatred of the Tory party... So far as I am concerned, they are lower than vermin.
Aneurin Bevan, on the entire Conservative Party

The Prime Minister has an absolute genius for putting flamboyant labels on empty luggage.
Aneurin Bevan, on Harold Macmillan

Tory shame was only slightly alleviated by Walter Monckton – and then they didn't know whether to wear him as a gas-mask or a jock-strap.
Aneurin Bevan, on Walter Monckton

I am not going to spend any time whatsoever in attacking the Foreign Secretary... If we complain about the tune, there is no reason to attack the monkey when the organ grinder is present.
Aneurin Bevan, on Anthony Eden, Prime Minister, and Selwyn Lloyd as Foreign Secretary.

Bevan also made a point of taking the time to be rude about other areas of life that were unlucky enough to catch his attention unfavourably.

This island is made mainly of coal and surrounded by fish. Only an organizing genius could produce a shortage of coal and fish at the same time.
Aneurin Bevan

We know what happens to people who stay in the middle of the road. They get run down.
Aneurin Bevan

You call that statesmanship? I call it an emotional spasm.
Aneurin Bevan

I read the newspapers avidly. It is my one form of continuous fiction.
Aneurin Bevan

Damn it all, you can't have the crown of thorns and the thirty pieces of silver.
Aneurin Bevan, on his own position in the Labour Party

As always, there were plenty of politicians and other commentators who disliked Bevan's stance, and were delighted to say so.

Bevan done and lost his friends – one quarter Bloody Revolutionary, one quarter Pacifist, one half "Same Policy as the Tories, but with jobs".
Lord Beaverbrook, 1879–1964, on Aneurin Bevan

He can hardly enter a railway train because there is no Fourth Class.
Daily Express newspaper, 1932, on Aneurin Bevan

He enjoys prophesying the imminent fall of the capitalist system, and is prepared to play a part, any part, in its burial, except that of mute.
Harold Macmillan, 1894–1986, on Aneurin Bevan

Clement Attlee entered Parliament in 1922, after serving in the First World War. By 1935, he had risen to leader of the Labour Party, and was Prime Minister from 1945 to 1951. Although his opponents frequently characterized him as bland and colourless, he did not get to be leader of a political party by being the shy and retiring type, and he was known to unleash scathing attacks when the situation warranted.

Why does Mosley always speak to us as though he were a feudal landlord abusing tenants who are in arrears with their rent?
Clement Attlee, 1883–1967, on Oswald Mosley

Always was a loud-mouthed fellow.
Clement Attlee, on Hugh Dalton

Queer bird, Halifax. Very humorous, all hunting and Holy Communion.
Clement Attlee, on Lord Halifax.

The voice we heard was that of Mr Churchill, but the mind was that of Lord Beaverbrook.
Clement Attlee, on Winston Churchill

A period of silence on your part would be welcome.
Clement Attlee, to Harold Laski, Chairman of the Labour Party

The press lives on disaster.
Clement Attlee

Democracy means government by discussion, but it is only effective if you can stop the people talking.
Clement Attlee

The illegitimate child of Karl Marx and Catherine the Great.
Clement Attlee, on Russian Communism

David Lloyd George was British Prime Minister between 1916 and 1922. He lost the support of much of his party, the Liberals, as a result of his foreign policy, particularly regarding Russia, Ireland and Turkey. He was also a dedicated foe of the House of Lords. They rejected a budget of his in 1909, and in return their power was legally limited some two years later ... perhaps as revenge.

The lean and trusty mastiff which is to watch over our interests, but which runs away at the first snarl of the trade unions... A mastiff? It is the right honourable gentleman's poodle.
David Lloyd George, 1863–1945, on the House of Lords and Arthur Balfour

A fully-equipped duke costs as much to keep up as two Dreadnoughts; and dukes are just as great a terror, and they last longer.
David Lloyd George

A body of five hundred men chosen at random from amongst the unemployed.
David Lloyd George, on the House of Lords

Lord Beaverbrook's butler: *"The Lord is out walking."*

Lloyd George: *"Ah, on the water, I presume."*

I would as soon go for a sunny evening stroll round Walton Heath with a grasshopper as try to work with Northcliffe.
David Lloyd George, on Lord Northcliffe.

It would be a mistake to assume that Lloyd George reserved all his disdain for the peerage, however. He also held plenty back for his colleagues...

Wild men, screaming through the keyholes.
David Lloyd George, on his fellow delegates at the Versailles Peace Conference

No more than the whiff of scent on a lady's pocket handkerchief.
David Lloyd George, on Arthur Balfour's historical significance

Neville has a retail mind in a wholesale business.
David Lloyd George, on Neville Chamberlain

The Prime Minister should give an example of sacrifice, because there is nothing which can contribute more to victory than that he should sacrifice the seals of office.
David Lloyd George, on Neville Chamberlain

He would make a drum out of the skin of his mother in order to sound his own praises.
David Lloyd George, on Winston Churchill

Sufficient conscience to bother him, but not sufficient to keep him straight.
David Lloyd George, on Ramsay Macdonald

One of those revolving lighthouses which radiate momentary gleams of light far out into the surrounding gloom, and then suddenly relapse into complete darkness. There were no intermediate stages.
David Lloyd George, on Lord Kitchener

He has sat on the fence so long the iron has entered into his soul.
David Lloyd George, on John Simon

...and for the rest of the world, too.

The world is becoming like a lunatic asylum run by lunatics.
David Lloyd George

Negotiating with de Valera is like trying to pick up mercury with a fork.
David Lloyd George, on Eamon de Valera, an Irish politician

Death is the most convenient time to tax rich people.
David Lloyd George

If you want to succeed in politics, you must keep your conscience firmly under control.
David Lloyd George

The government are behaving like a bevy of maiden aunts who have fallen among buccaneers.
David Lloyd George, on the government's response to the Spanish Civil War

Like most other vocal public figures, Lloyd George had plenty of rivals and opponents who were only too happy to bite back.

He could not see a belt without hitting below it.
Margot Asquith, 1864–1945, on Lloyd George

He would have a better rating in British mythology if he had shared the fate of Abraham Lincoln.
John Grigg, 1924–, on Lloyd George

This goat-footed bard, this half-human visitor to our age from the hag-ridden magic and enchanted woods of Celtic antiquity.
John Maynard Keynes,1883–1946, *Essays and Sketches in Biography*, on Lloyd George

He spent his whole life in plastering together the true and the false and therefrom manufacturing the plausible.
Standley Baldwin (after Thomas Carlyle), 1867–1947, on Lloyd George

He didn't care which direction the car was travelling, so long as he remained in the driver's seat.
Lord Beaverbrook, 1879–1964, on Lloyd George

Remembered as a Liberal politician, William Gladstone started off as a Tory but defected, and was subsequently four times Prime Minister, which may say something about politics. He twice resigned as PM after Home Rule bills that he introduced were defeated. He was a powerful political influence, and his shadow was felt long after his death. He particularly disapproved of Turkish Moslem aggression against native Christians.

Let the Turks now carry away their abuses in the only possible manner, namely by carrying off themselves ... one and all, bag and baggage, shall I hope clear out from the province that they have desolated and profaned.
William Gladstone, 1809–1898

Ireland, Ireland! That cloud in the west, that coming storm.
William Gladstone

We have been borne down in a torrent of gin and beer.
William Gladstone, on the British public.

The blubbering cabinet.
William Gladstone, on his ministers at his final cabinet meeting.

There never was a Churchill from John of Marlborough down that had either morals or principles.
William Gladstone, on Lord Randolph Churchill, Sir Winston's father.

If Gladstone was inclined to be rude at times, it was nothing compared to the volume of invective that he incited from others. Like Attlee, he attracted far more venom than he released. Benjamin Disraeli particularly loathed the man.

Gladstone appears to me one of the contemptiblest men I ever looked on. A poor Ritualist; an almost spectral kind of phantasm of a man, nothing in him but forms and ceremonies and outside wrappings.
Thomas Carlyle, 1795–1881, on William Gladstone

An old man in a hurry.
Randolph Churchill, 1849–1895, on William Gladstone

He speaks to me as if I were a public meeting.
Queen Victoria, 1819–1901, on William Gladstone.

An old, wild and incomprehensible man.
Queen Victoria, on William Gladstone

If Glastone fell into the Thames, that would be a misfortune, and if anybody pulled him out, that would be a calamity.
Benjamin Disraeli, 1804–1881, on how to quantify disasters

When you have to deal with an earnest man, severely religious and enthusiastic, every attempted arrangement ends in unintelligible correspondence and violated confidence.
Benjamin Disraeli, on William Gladstone

He has not a single redeeming defect.
Benjamin Disraeli, on William Gladstone

Posterity will do justice to that unprincipled maniac Gladstone, an extraordinary mixture of envy, vindictiveness, hypocrisy, and superstition; and with one commanding characteristic, whether Prime Minister or Leader of Opposition, whether preaching, praying, speechifying or scribbling, never a gentleman!
Benjamin Disraeli, on William Gladstone

Inebriated with the exuberance of his own verbosity, and gifted with an egotistical imagination.
Benjamin Disraeli, on William Gladstone

What restlessness! What vanity! And what unhappiness must be his! Easy to say he is mad. It looks it.
Benjamin Disraeli, on William Gladstone

Although he was particularly unpleasant about Gladstone, Disraeli unleashed his wit at a great number of other targets. A popular novelist before entering Parliament as an unashamedly imperialist Conservative, it was his rhetoric that won him leadership of the party after his attacks brought down Robert Peel's Conservative government – his own party. Truly there are no friends in politics.

He is a burglar of others' intellect... There is no statesman who has committed political larceny on so great a scale.
Benjamin Disraeli, on Robert Peel

He traces the steam engine always back to the tea-kettle.
Benjamin Disraeli, on Robert Peel

Wanting imagination he lacked prescience. His judgement was faultless provided he had not to deal with the future.
Benjamin Disraeli, on Robert Peel

The right honourable gentleman is reminiscent of a poker. The only difference is that a poker gives off occasional signs of warmth.
Benjamin Disraeli, on Robert Peel

The right honourable gentleman's smile is like the silver fittings on a coffin.
Benjamin Disraeli, on Robert Peel

A Conservative Government is an organized hypocrisy.
Benjamin Disraeli, on Peel's government.

He has to learn that petulance is not sarcasm, and that insolence is not invective.
Benjamin Disraeli, on Charles Wood

He is a great master of gibes and flouts and jeers.
Benjamin Disraeli, on Lord Salisbury

We have legalized confiscation, consecrated sacrilege, and condoned high treason.
Benjamin Disraeli, on Gladstone's policy on Ireland

As I sat opposite the Treasury Bench, the ministers reminded me of one of those marine landscapes not very unusual on the coasts of South America. You

behold a range of exhausted volcanoes, not a flame flickers on a single pallid crest, but the situation is still dangerous. There are occasional earthquakes, and ever and anon the dark rumbling of the sea.
Benjamin Disraeli, on the Liberal Party

Everyone likes flattery; and when you come to Royalty, you should lay it on with a trowel.
Benjamin Disraeli, on Queen Victoria

There are three kinds of lies: lies, damned lies and statistics.
Benjamin Disraeli, on the art of politics.

Disraeli used his popular novels extensively to further his political views, attacking established practices and the art of politics in general – perhaps with the aim of winning the admiration of the public. His high profile certainly did not hamper his leadership bid.

There is no act of treachery or meanness of which a political party is not capable; for in politics there is no honour.
Benjamin Disraeli, *Vivian Grey*

The Lords do not encourage wit, and so are obliged to put up with pertness.
Benjamin Disraeli, *The Young Duke*

The practice of politics in the East may be defined by one word – dissimulation.
Benjamin Disraeli, *Contarini Fleming*

A government of statesmen or of clerks? Of Humbug or Humdrum?
Benjamin Disraeli, *Coningsby*

We owe the English peerage to three sources: the spoilation of the Church; the open and flagrant sale of honours by the elder Stuarts; and the borough-mongering of our own time.
Ibid.

Conservatism discards prescription, shrinks from principle, disavows progress; having rejected all respect for antiquity, it offers no redress for the present, and makes no preparation for the future.
Ibid.

I*t seems to me a barren thing, this Conservatism – an unhappy cross-breed, the mule of politics that engenders nothing.*
Ibid.

Where can we find faith in a nation of secretaries?
Ibid.

Often remembered as the man who purchased the Polaris missile system and defended the British nuclear arsenal, Harold Macmillan was a Conservative politician and Prime Minister. With a dry sense of humour rather than a scathing one, he was something of an acquired taste – one that several of his contemporaries plainly did not take the effort to appreciate.

Revolt by all means; but only on one issue at a time. To do more would be to confuse the whips.
Harold Macmillan, 1894–1986, advising new MPs

The only quality needed for an MP is the ability to write a good letter.
Harold Macmillan, on the abilities of politicians

As usual, the Liberals offer a mixture of sound and original ideas. Unfortunately none of the sound ideas is original and none of the original ideas is sound.
Harold Macmillan

A successful [current affairs] television show seems to be more and more a cross between a music-hall turn and a scene in a torture chamber.
Harold Macmillan, on politics in the media

Forever poised between a cliché and an indiscretion.
Harold Macmillan, on being Foreign Secretary

It was almost impossible to believe he was anything but a down-at-heel actor resting between engagements at the decrepit theatres of minor provincial towns.
Bernard Levin, 1928–, on Harold Macmillan

The stag at bay with the mentality of the fox at large.
Bernard Levin, on Harold Macmillan

He is very clever and takes infinite pains to make himself well informed – but somehow I doubt whether he will ever make much political progress. He bores people too quickly, and has little or no sense of humour.
Cuthbert Headlam, 1876–1964, on Harold Macmillan

The right honourable gentleman has inherited the streak of charlatanry in Disraeli without his vision, and the self-righteousness of Gladstone without his dedication to principle.
Harold Wilson, 1916–1995, on Harold Macmillan

Wilson himself was a well-practised verbal warrior. His time as Prime Minster on behalf of the Labour Party was complicated by the difficulties surrounding British entry into the European Community, trade union disputes, and economic troubles. Sadly, he is not widely remembered for perhaps his greatest achievement – setting up the Open University, a well-respected institution that does all its teaching via late-night television and correspondence courses, making education truly egalitarian.

He immatures with age.
Harold Wilson, 1916–1995, on Tony Benn

The Smethwick Conservatives can have the satisfaction of having topped the poll, and of having sent here as their Member one who, until a further General Election restores him to oblivion, will serve his term here as a parliamentary leper.
Harold Wilson, on a by-election winner with alleged racist connections

All the little gnomes in Zurich and the other financial centres about whom we keep on hearing.
Harold Wilson, on the merchant banking trade

This party is a bit like an old stagecoach. If you drive along at a rapid rate, everyone aboard is either so exhilarated or so seasick that you don't have a lot of difficulty.
Harold Wilson, on how to lead the Labour Party

Whichever party is in office, the Treasury is in power.
Harold Wilson

After half a century of democratic advance, the whole process has ground to a halt with a Fourteenth Earl.
Harold Wilson, on Sir Alec Douglas-Home

Not all of Wilson's colleagues were completely convinced of the humble, poverty-stricken roots he made such a big issue about. Others had plenty to say, too.

As far as the 14th Earl is concerned, I suppose that Mr Wilson, when you come to think of it, is the 14th Mr Wilson.
Sir Alec Douglas-Home, 1903–1995, on Harold Wilson

If Harold Wilson ever went to school without any boots, it was merely because he was too big for them.
Harold Macmillan, 1894–1986, on Harold Wilson

No-one could accuse himself of courage more often than the Prime Minister.
Nigel Birch, 1906–1981, on Harold Wilson

He's going around the country stirring up apathy.
William Whitelaw, 1918–, on Harold Wilson

He's just a little man who has been stupid.
Lord George-Brown, 1914–1985, on Harold Wilson

More recently, Margaret Thatcher has been one of the most controversial British politicians in the last 50 years. Sometimes wildly popular, other times wildly unpopular, the first female Prime Minister was staunchly Conservative, with hard-line, right-wing views and a completely uncompromising attitude. She was forthright and outspoken, and did not shrink from critical appraisals.

You don't reach Downing Street by pretending you've travelled the road to Damascus when you haven't even left home.
Margaret Thatcher, 1925 –, on Neil Kinnock

In politics, if you want anything said, ask a man. If you want anything done, ask a woman.
Margaret Thatcher

I don't mind how much my ministers talk, as long as they do what I say.
Margaret Thatcher

Treachery with a smile on its face.
Margaret Thatcher, on her removal as Prime Minister

I've got no hang-ups about my background, like you intellectual commentators in the south-east.
Margaret Thatcher

It's exciting to have a real crisis on your hands, when you have spent half your political life dealing with humdrum issues like the environment.
Margaret Thatcher, on the Falklands War

One of the things that politics has taught me is that men are not a reasoned or reasonable sex.
Margaret Thatcher

Her critics, however, were far more "forthright and outspoken". While some of them attacked her stances, ideals and policies, others were directly and personally offensive.

Jezebel.
Rev. Ian Paisley, 1926 –, on Margaret Thatcher

Attila the Hen.
Clement Freud, 1924 –, on Margaret Thatcher

I wouldn't say she is open-minded on the Middle East so much as empty-headed. She probably thinks Sinai is the plural of Sinus.
Jonathan Aitken, 1942 –, on Margaret Thatcher

The Immaculate Misconception
Norman St John-Stevas, 1929 –, on Margaret Thatcher

David Owen in drag.
The *Rhodesia Herald* newspaper, 1984, on Margaret Thatcher

The great she-elephant.
Julian Critchley, 1930 –, on Margaret Thatcher

If she has a weakness it is for shopkeepers, which probably accounts for the fact that she cannot pass a branch of Marks and Spencers without inviting the manager to join her private office.
Julian Critchley, on Margaret Thatcher

She cannot see an institution without hitting it with her handbag.
Julian Critchley, on Margaret Thatcher

She is happier getting in and out of tanks than in and out of museums or theatre seats. She seems to derive more pleasure from admiring new missiles than great works of art. What else can we expect from an ex-Spam hoarder from Grantham presiding over the social and economic decline of the country?
Julian Critchley, on Margaret Thatcher

The nanny appeared to be extinct until 1975, when, like the coelacanth, she suddenly and unexpectedly reappeared in the shape of Margaret Thatcher.
Simon Hoggart, 1946 –, on Margaret Thatcher

She sounded like the Book of Revelations *read out over a railway station public address system by a headmistress of a certain age wearing calico knickers.*
Clive James, 1939 –, on Margaret Thatcher

A perfectly good second-class chemist, a Beta chemist, she wasn't an interesting person, except as a Conservative. I would never, if I had amusing, interesting people staying, have thought of asking Margaret Thatcher.
Dame Janet Vaughn, 1892–1975, on Margaret Thatcher

Rhoda the Rhino.
Denis Healey, 1917 –, on Margaret Thatcher

The Prime Minister tells us she has given the French president a piece of her mind – not a gift I would receive with alacrity.
Denis Healey, on Margaret Thatcher

Pétain in petticoats.
Denis Healey, on Margaret Thatcher

She approaches the problems of our country with all the one-dimensional subtlety of a comic strip.
Denis Healey, on Margaret Thatcher

And who is the Mephistopheles behind this shabby Faust? To quote her own backbenchers, the Great She-Elephant, She-Who-Must-Be-Obeyed, the Catherine the Great of Finchley, the Prime Minister herself.
Denis Healey, on Margaret Thatcher and her Foreign Secretary, Geoffrey Howe

While the rest of Europe is marching to confront the new challenges, the Prime Minister is shuffling along in the gutter in the opposite direction, like an old bag lady, muttering imprecations at anyone who catches her eye.
Denis Healey, on Margaret Thatcher

Hopping over the Atlantic, we find that the members of the US political scene have been more restrained about each other than their British counterparts. They have often been far more critical of the system itself, however. Exactly what this says about the differences between the British and American psyches is left to the reader...

Henry L. Mencken was variously described as "the most powerful man in America" (according to the *New York Times*) and as a public nuisance – or far, far worse – but there is no doubt he possessed a great gift for unpleasantly acidic wit. A journalist, commentator and critic, he was never seen without his trademark cigar. A bachelor for most of his life, he still remained popular with women; when he finally married at the age of 50, the popular press gloated over his fall into matrimony. His comments on political indviduals were almost invariably negative, and sharply so.

He slept more than any other president, whether by day or by night. Nero fiddled, but Coolidge only snored.
Henry L. Mencken, 1880–1956, on Calvin Coolidge

If there had been any formidable body of cannibals in the country he would have promised to provide them with free missionaries, fattened at the taxpayer's expense.
Henry L. Mencken, on Harry Truman's 1948 presidential campaign

He sailed through American history like a steel ship loaded with monoliths of granite.
Henry L. Mencken, on Grover Cleveland

He writes the worst English that I have ever encountered. It reminds me of a string of wet sponges; it reminds me of tattered washing on the line; it reminds me of stale bean soup, of college yells, of dogs barking through endless nights.

It is so bad that a sort of grandeur creeps into it. It drags itself out of the dark abyss (I was about to write abscess) of pish and crawls insanely up the topmost pinnacle of the posh. It is rumble and bumble. It is flap and doodle. It is balder and dash.
Henry L. Mencken, on Warren G. Harding

A tin horn politician with the manner of a rural corn doctor and the mien of a ham actor.
Henry L. Mencken, on Warren G. Harding

One always thinks of him as a glorified bouncer engaged eternally in cleaning out bar-rooms and not too proud to gouge when the inspiration came to him, or to bite in the clinches.
Henry L Mencken, on Theodore Roosevelt

As vicious as he was about specific people, Mencken was every bit as unpleasant about the field of politics as a whole, and about the plight of mankind.

Puritanism: the haunting fear that someone, somewhere may be happy.
Henry L. Mencken, *Chrestomathy*

No one in this world, so far as I know – and I have searched the records for years, and employed agents to help me – has ever lost money by underestimating the intelligence of the great masses of the plain people.
Henry L. Mencken, on exploitation

The whole aim of practical politics is to keep the populace alarmed – and hence clamorous to be led to safety – by menacing it with an endless series of hobgoblins, all of them imaginary.
Henry L. Mencken, *In Defence Of Women*

The worst government is often the most moral. One composed of cynics is often vey tolerant and humane. But when fanatics are on top, there is no limit to oppression.
Henry L. Mencken, *Minority Report*

A government can never be the impersonal thing described in text-books. It is simply a group of men like any other. In every 100 of the men composing it there are two who are honest and intelligent, ten obvious scoundrels, and 88 poor fish.
Henry L. Mencken

Under democracy one party always devotes its chief energies to trying to prove that the other party is unfit to rule – and both commonly succeed, and are right.
Henry L. Mencken

Unsurprisingly for someone spending so much time being critical of others, Mencken attracted a large volume of very bitter insults. Some, frankly, are so offensive as to be quite spectacular...

Mencken, with his filthy verbal haemorrhages, is so low down in the moral scale, so damnable dirty, so vile and degenerate, that when his time comes to die, it will take a special dispensation from Heaven to get him into the bottommost pit of Hell.
Letter to the *Jackson News* newspaper, 1934, on H.L. Mencken

With a pig's eyes that never look up, with a pig's snout that loves muck, with a pig's brain that knows only the sty, and a pig's squeal that cries only when he is hurt, he sometimes opens his pig's mouth, tusked and ugly, and lets out the voice of God, railing at the whitewash that covers the manure of his habitat.
William White, 1906–, on H.L. Mencken

Mr Mencken did not degenerate from an ape, but an ass. And in the process of evolution *the tail was eliminated, the ears became shorter, and the hind parts smaller; but the ability to bray was increased, intensified, amplified, and otherwise assified about one million times.*
J.D. Tedder, 1890–1967, on H.L. Mencken

Mr Mencken talks about truth as if she were his mistress, but he handles her like an iceman.
Stuart Sherman, 1868–1944, on H.L. Mencken

Henry Kissinger was also known for his razor-sharp wit. German-born, he worked for American military intelligence in Germany, and followed this up with superb results academically at Harvard. Later, his secret work in China and Russia led to Nixon's visits to both countries; in 1973 he shared the Nobel Peace Prize. Ironically for a politician who devoted himself to diplomacy and defusing crises, he frequently showed a mean streak.

The illegal we do immediately. The unconstitutional takes a little longer.
Henry Kissinger, 1923 –

Ninety percent of the politicians give the other ten percent a bad name.
Henry Kissinger

History has so far shown us only two roads to international stability: equilibrium and domination.
Henry Kissinger

An Iranian moderate is one who has run out of ammunition.
Henry Kissinger

For Wilson, the justification of America's international role was messianic: America had an obligation not to the balance of power, but to spread its principles throughout the world.
Henry Kissinger, on Woodrow Wilson

There cannot be a crisis next week. My schedule is already full.
Henry Kissinger

The main advantage of being famous is that when you bore people at dinner parties they think it is their fault.
Henry Kissinger

Born in Canada and broadly critical of several key tenets of economic theory, American economist John Kenneth Galbraith believed that affluent societies were imbalanced. Economic growth is widely considered a good thing – but Galbraith asked why, exactly, and argued instead that the State should help support the people, condemning the tendency of capitalism to create broad gaps between the rich and the poor. Given this doctrine, it will be no surprise that he was extremely hostile towards various aspects of political and economic life.

Trickle-down theory – the less than elegant metaphor that if one feeds the horse enough oats, some will pass through to the road for the sparrows.
John Kenneth Galbraith, 1908–, *The Culture of Contentment*

In a community where public services have failed to keep abreast of private consumption things are very different. Here, in an atmosphere of private opulence and public squalor, the private goods have full sway.
John Kenneth Galbraith, *The Affluent Society*

These are the days when men of all social disciplines and all political faiths seek the comfortable and the accepted; when the man of controversy is looked upon as

a disturbing influence; when originality is taken to be a mark of instability; and when, in minor modification of the scriptural parable, the bland lead the bland.
Ibid.

The greater the wealth, the thicker will be the dirt.
Ibid.

The reduction of politics to a spectator sport has been one of the more malign accomplishments of television. Television newsmen are breathless on how the game is being played, largely silent on what the game is all about.
John Kenneth Galbraith, *A Life in Our Times*

In public administration good sense would seem to require the public expectation be kept at the lowest possible level in order to minimize eventual diasppointment.
Ibid.

The experience of being disastrously wrong is salutary; no economist should be denied it, and not many are.
Ibid.

One of the little-celebrated powers of Presidents (and other high government officials) is to listen to their critics with just enough sympathy to ensure their silence.
Ibid.

Politics is not the art of the possible. It consists in choosing between the disastrous and the unpalatable.
John Kenneth Galbraith, to President J.F. Kennedy

A Hollywood actor turned politician, President Ronald Reagan's time in office was marked by fundamentalist speeches, aggressive foreign policy and increased military spending – so much so that even social cuts couldn't reverse the increasing debt. Detractors were as likely to make reference to his film career as to his political position, and towards the end of his second term there was much speculation in the popular media regarding his mental health. Despite this, he remained a wry commentator on political life.

My fellow Americans, I am pleased to tell you I just signed legislation which outlaws Russia forever. The bombing begins in five minutes.
Ronald Reagan, 1911–, said whimsically during a microphone test

I don't resent his popularity or anything else. Good Lord, I co-starred with Errol Flynn once.
Ronald Reagan, on Mikhail Gorbachev

The mad dog of the Middle East.
Ronald Reagan, on Colonel Gadaffi

We are especially not going to tolerate these attacks from outlaw states run by the strangest collection of misfits, Looney Tunes and squalid criminals since the advent of the Third Reich.
Ronald Reagan, spoken after the terrorist hijacking of a US plane

The nine most terrifying words in the English language are: "I'm from the government and I'm here to help."
Ronald Reagan

Government does not solve problems; it subsidises them.
Ronald Reagan

I've noticed that everybody who is for abortion has already been born.
Ronald Reagan

Politics is supposed to be the second oldest profession. I have come to realize that it bears a very close resemblance to the first.
Ronald Reagan

Although opponents were quick to latch onto most of Reagan's idiosyncrasies, it was his age that attracted the greatest amount of unwanted attention.

A triumph of the embalmer's art.
Gore Vidal, 1925–, on Ronald Reagan

Ronald Reagan doesn't dye his hair – he's just prematurely orange.
Gerald Ford, 1913–, on Ronald Reagan

The first man in twenty years to make the Presidency a part-time job, a means of filling up a few of the otherwise blank days of retirement.
Simon Hoggart, 1946–, on Ronald Reagan

Reagan won because he stood against Jimmy Carter. If he'd run unopposed, he would have lost.
Mort Sahl, 1926–, on Ronald Reagan

He is attempting a great breakthrough in political technology – he has been perfecting the Teflon-coated Presidency. He sees to it that nothing sticks to him.
Patricia Schroeder, 1940–, on Ronald Reagan

We've got the kind of President who thinks arms control means some kind of deodorant.
Patricia Schroeder, on Ronald Reagan

Ronald Reagan – the president who never told bad news to the American people.
Garrison Keillor, 1942–, on Ronald Reagan

The founding fathers of America were generally grave, serious-minded men not much given to the spiteful excesses of their European colleagues. Thomas Jefferson, who founded the Democratic Republican Party and drafted most of the Declaration of Independence, reserved most of his scorn for the system and its effect on mankind.

Experience declares that man is the only animal which devours its own kind, for I can apply no milder term to the governments of Europe, and to the general prey of the rich on the poor.
Thomas Jefferson, 1743–1826, private correspondence

If I could not go to Heaven but with a party, I would not go there at all.
Thomas Jefferson, private correspondence, on political affiliations

Merchants have no country. The mere spot they stand on does not constitute so strong an attachment as that from which they draw their gains.
Thomas Jefferson, private correspondence

Millions of innocent men, women, and children, since the introduction of Christianity, have been burnt, tortured, fined, imprisoned; yet we have not advanced one inch towards uniformity. What has been the effect of coercion? To make one half of the world fools, and the other half hypocrites.
Thomas Jefferson, *Notes on the State of Virginia*, on religious discussion

We are all Republicans – we are all Federalists. If there be any among us who would wish to dissolve this Union or to change its republican form, let them stand undisturbed as monuments of the safety with which error of opinion may be tolerated where reason is left free to combat it.
Thomas Jefferson, *First Inaugural Address*

Were we directed from Washington when to sow, and when to reap, we should soon want bread.
Thomas Jefferson, *Autobiography*

A cold-blooded, calculating, uncprincipled usurper, without a virtue; no statesman, knowing nothing of commerce, political economy, or civil government, and supplying ignorance by bold presumption.
Thomas Jefferson, on Napoleon Bonaparte

Jefferson's critics did not display the same restraint when it came to slating the man. In particular, the first of the following quotes could be considered a rather sensational, alarmist reaction to his election...

Murder, robbery, rape, adultery and incest will be openly taught and practised, the air will be rent with cries of distress, the soil soaked with blood, and the nation black with crimes. Where is the heart that can contemplate such a scene without shivering with horror?
New England Courant newspaper, 1801, on the election of Thomas Jefferson

The moral character of Jefferson was repulsive. Continually puling about liberty, equality and the degrading curse of slavery, he brought his own children to the hammer, and made money of his debaucheries.
Alexander Hamilton, 1755–1804, on Thomas Jefferson

A slur upon the moral government of the world.
John Quincy Adams, 1767–1848, on Thomas Jefferson

I cannot live in this miserable, undone country, where, as the Turks follow their sacred standard, which is a pair of Mahomet's breeches, we are governed by the old red breeches of the prince of projectors, St. Thomas of Cantingbury.
John Randolph, 1773–1833, on Thomas Jefferson's Presidency

When Abraham Lincoln was elected as President in 1861, the Southern states that still used slaves dropped out of the Union, an act which led to the Civil War and the complete abolition of slavery. Five days after winning the war, Lincoln was assassinated. As might be expected of such a divisive figure, a lot of unpleasant insults were thrown his way.

God damn your God damned old hellfired God damned soul to hell. God damn you and God damn your God damned family's God damned hellfired God damned soul to hell and Good damnation God damn them and God damn your God damned friends to hell.
Peter Muggins, US citizen, 1812–1877, expressing his heartfelt irritation in a letter to Abraham Lincoln

Filthy story-teller, despot, liar, thief, braggart, buffoon, usurper, monster, ignoramus Abe, old scoundrel, perjurer, robber, swindler, tyrant, field-butcher, land-pirate.
Harper's Weekly magazine, 1852, on Abraham Lincoln

King Abraham charging at the head of his victorious legions, and joking even in the heat of battle, is a thought to terrifying to dwell on. Let us hope that it is only imagination ... that if the great Abraham is to join the headless procession his ugly visage will be removed by his own betrayed countrymen – by the men whose rights he has denied, whose persons he has immured in his loathsome bastilles, whose sons and brothers he has murdered upon Southern battlefields – by that nation which the whole world despises now, because they regard this Buffoon as its type.
John Esten Cooke, 1856–1919, on Abraham Lincoln

His soul seems made of leather, and incapable of any grand or noble emotion. Compared with the mass of men, he is a line of flat prose in a beautiful and spirited lyric. He lowers, he never elevates you. When he hits upon a policy, substantially good in itself, he contrives to belittle it, besmear it in some way to render it mean, contemptible and useless. Even wisdom from him seems but folly.
New York Post newspaper, 1853, on Abraham Lincoln

Nothing more than a well-meaning baboon.
General McClellan, 1826–1885, on Abraham Lincoln

I went to the White House directly after tea where I found "the original Gorilla" about as intelligent as ever. What a specimen to be at the head of our affairs now!
Ibid., on Abraham Lincoln

An offensive exhibition of boorishness and vulgarity.
Chicago Times newspaper, 1857, on Abraham Lincoln

Our country owes all our troubles to him, and God simply made me an instrument of his punishment.
John Wilkes Booth, 1838–1865, on his assassination of Abraham Lincoln

This man's appearance, his pedigree, his coarse low jokes and anecdotes, his vulgar similes and his frivolity, are a disgrace to the seat he holds.
Ibid., on Abraham Lincoln

Characteristically, Lincoln himself saved the bulk of his negative opinions for more abstract targets, such as politics and slavery.

Politicians are a set of men who have interests aside from the interests of the people, and who, to say the most of them, are, taken as a mass, at least one long step removed from honest men.
Abraham Lincoln, 1809–1865

Whenever I hear anyone arguing for slavery, I feel a strong impulse to see it tried on him personally.
Abraham Lincoln

People who like this sort of thing will find that this is the sort of thing they like.
Abraham Lincoln, playing literary critic

The Lord prefers common-looking people. That is why he makes so many of them.
Abraham Lincoln

Henry Clay was a powerful figure in nineteenth-century American politics. Although he never made president, he stood three times, and was a dominant leader of the House of Representatives. A significant force, he tried repeatedly to hold the Union together. He was strongly critical of Andrew Jackson, who returned the favour.

The arts of power and its minions are the same in all countries and in all ages. It marks a victim; denounces it; and excites the public odium and the public hatred to conceal its own abuses and encroachments.
Henry Clay, 1777–1852

Their disappearance from the human family will be no great loss to the world.
Henry Clay, on Native Americans

A rigid, fanatic, ambitious, selfishly partizan and sectional turncoat with too much genius and too little common sense, who will either die a traitor or a madman.
Henry Clay, on John Calhoun

I cannot believe that the killing of two thousand Englishmen at New Orleans qualifies a person for the various difficult and complicated duties of the presidency.
Henry Clay, on Andrew Jackson

He is ignorant, passionate, hypocritical, corrupt and easily swayed by the basest men who surround him.
Henry Clay, on Andrew Jackson.

He is certainly the basest, meanest scoundrel that ever disgraced the image of God – nothing too mean or low for him to condescend to.
Andrew Jackson, 1767–1845, on Henry Clay

I didn't shoot Henry Clay, and I didn't hang John Calhoun.
Andrew Jackson, on the things he left undone in his life

He prefers the specious to the solid, and the plausible to the true ... he is a bad man, an imposter, a creator of wicked schemes.
John Calhoun, 1782–1850, on Henry Clay

He is, like almost all the eminent men of this country, only half educated. His morals, public and private, are loose.
John Quincy Adams, 1767–1848, on Henry Clay

No-one knew better than the Cock of Kentucky which side his bread was buttered on: and he liked his butter. A considerable portion of his public life was spent in trying to find butter for both sides of the slice.
Irving F. Stone, 1907–1989, on Henry Clay

Adlai Stevenson, a Democrat politician with a reputation for honesty and plain talking, was a vigorous anti-corruption crusader. Twice the presidential candidate, he lost out both times to Eisenhower. The cynical might wonder if it wasn't his straightforward manner that ensured his defeats...

I suppose flattery hurts no one, that is, if he doesn't inhale.
Adlai Stevenson, 1900–1965

The General has dedicated himself so many times, he must feel like the cornerstone of a public building.
Adlai Stevenson, on Dwight Eisenhower

In America any boy may become President, and I suppose that's just one of the risks he takes!
Adlai Stevenson

If they will stop telling lies about the Democrats, we will stop telling the truth about them.
Adlai Stevenson, on the Republican party

A cold, arrogant and ruthless man who has been exhausting himself running around the world because he really trusts no one.
Adlai Stevenson, on John Foster Dulles

A life long servant of the most materialistic forces in our society, a Big Lawyer for the Big Money, a pre-war apologist for Japanese aggression and Nazi expansion, an exponent of Machiavellianism so long as the Axis was winning, and advocate of Christian peace as soon as its defeat was forseen, Mr Dulles by his constant invocation of Christianity and freedom has succeeded in making these ideals suspect in the minds of uncommitted millions who hear in them only the tom-toms beating for a new war.
Adlai Stevenson, on John Foster Dulles

We hear the Secretary of State boasting of his brinkmanship – the art of bringing us to the edge of the abyss.
Adlai Stevenson, on John Foster Dulles

The sound of tireless voices is the price we pay for the right to hear the music of our own opinions.
Adlai Stevenson

A politician is a person who approaches every subject with an open mouth.
Adlai Stevenson

The kind of politician who would cut down a redwood tree and then mount the stump to make a speech for conservation.
Adlai Stevenson, on Richard Nixon

Nixonland is a land of slander and scare, of lay innuendo, of a poison pen and the anonymous telephone call, and hustling, pushing and thieving, the land of smash and grab and anything to win.
Adlai Stevenson, on Richard Nixon

Nixon seems to equate criticism with subversion and being hard on Republicans to being soft on Communism.
Adlai Stevenson, on Richard Nixon

Stevenson, of course, was just one of many who queued to pay their disrespects to Nixon. Tricky Dicky, slung out of the presidency for his dishonesty and dubious behaviour, attracted a lot of malign commentary even before his impeachment. He acknowledged that his fall was his own fault – "I gave them a sword, and they stuck it in me" – but that didn't stop the critics from acknowledging it too, and often loudly.

The Eichmann trial taught the world the banality of evil, now Nixon is teaching the world the evil of banality.
J.F. Stone, 1907–1989, on Richard Nixon

Give me two weeks.
Dwight Eisenhower, 1890–1969, on how long it would take to sum up Vice-President Nixon's "contributions" to the presidential campaign

Nixon's motto was "if two wrongs don't make a right, try three".
Norman Cousins, 1915–1990, on Richard Nixon

If he wants to do his country a favour, he'll stay over there.
Barry Goldwater, 1909–, on Nixon's trip to China

Nixon impeached himself. He gave us Gerald Ford as his revenge.
Bella Abzug, 1920–, on Richard Nixon

When the cold light of history looks back on Richard Nixon's five years of unrestrained power in the White House, it will show that he had the same effect on Conservative/Republican politics as Charles Manson and the Hell's Angels had on hippies and flower power.
Hunter Thompson, 1939–, *The Great Shark Hunt*, on Richard Nixon

A monument to all the rancid genes and broken chromosomes that corrupt the possibilities of the American Dream.
Ibid., on Richard Nixon

He was a foul caricature of himself, a man with no soul, no inner convictions, with the integrity of a hyena and the style of a poison toad.
Ibid., on Richard Nixon

Although he died two years before Nixon was forced to resign, Harry Truman had long been complaining about the Republican and his lack of honesty. Nixon wasn't the only person who Truman was unpleasant about. He was frequently open with his negative opinions – as you would expect of the man who dropped the atom bomb on the Japanese.

I don't think the son of a bitch knows the difference between truth and lying.
Harry S. Truman, 1884–1972, on Richard Nixon

He is a shifty, goddamn, lying son of a bitch, and people knew it. He's one of the few in the history of the country to run for high office talking out of both sides of his mouth at the same time – and lying out of both sides.
Harry S. Truman, on Richard Nixon

Richard Nixon is a no-good lying bastard. He can lie out of both sides of his mouth at the same time and if he ever caught himself telling the truth, he'd lie just to keep his hand in.
Harry S. Truman, on Richard Nixon

I didn't fire him because he was a dumb son of a bitch, although he was, but that's not against the law for generals. If it was, half to three-quarters of them would be in jail.
Harry S. Truman, on General MacArthur

I never give them hell. I just tell the truth and they think it is hell.
Harry S. Truman, on the public's response to his open style

Pierce didn't know what was going on, and even if he had, he wouldn't have known what to do about it.
Harry S. Truman, on Franklin Pierce

The real trouble with Stevenson is that he's no better than a regular sissy.
Harry S. Truman, on Adlai Stevenson

Perhaps latching on to his "everyman" style, Truman's critics tended to characterize him as an ordinary man – perhaps a little *too* ordinary...

He is a man totally unfitted for the position.
John Lewis, 1880–1969, on Harry Truman as president

His principles are elastic, and he is careless with the truth. He has no special knowledge of any subject, and he is a malignant, scheming sort of individual who is dangerous not only to the United Mine Workers, but dangerous to the United States of America.
John Lewis, on Harry Truman

Truman proves that old adage that any man can become President of the United States.
Norman Thomas, 1884–1968, on Harry Truman

Among his many weaknesses was his utter inability to discriminate between history and histrionics.
Anonymous, on Harry Truman, quoted in *Reminiscences* by General MacArthur

I am against government by crony.
Harold Ickes, 1874–1952, on why he resigned from Truman's cabinet

A Southern Democrat, Lyndon Baines Johnson was Kennedy's Vice-President and took over after the assassination. Although he forced civil rights bills through Congress, he also upped American involvement in Vietnam. For a politician, he could be pretty blunt – there was never any doubt about when he was being offensive.

Son, in politics you've got to learn that overnight chicken shit can turn into chicken salad.
Lyndon B. Johnson, 1908–1973, when asked why he was pleasant to Richard Nixon

You know when you're milking a cow and you have all that foamy white milk in the bucket and you're just about through when all of a sudden the cow swishes her tail through a pile of manure and slaps it into that foamy white milk? Well, that's Bill Fullbright.
Lyndon B. Johnson, on William Fullbright

Better to have him inside the tent pissing out than outside pissing in.
Lyndon B. Johnson, on J. Edgar Hoover

Gerry Ford is so dumb he can't fart and chew gum at the same time.
Lyndon B. Johnson, on Gerald Ford

Gerry Ford is a nice guy, but he played too much football with his helmet off.
Lyndon B. Johnson, on Gerald Ford

If he was rude about opponents – and he certainly was – then Johnson was not much more polite about allies, staff, or his own policies ... as his critics observed.

The enviably attractive nephew who sings an Irish ballad for the company and then winsomely disappears before the table-clearing and dishwashing begin.
Lyndon B. Johnson, on John F. Kennedy's assassination

Did you ever think that making a speech in economics is like pissing down your leg? It seems hot to you, but it never does anything to anyone else.
Lyndon B. Johnson, to John K. Galbraith

We're not about to send American boys 9 or 10,000 miles away from home to do what Asian boys ought to be doing for themselves.
Lyndon B. Johnson, on Vietnam

I don't want loyalty, I want loyalty. *I want him to kiss my ass in Macy's window at high noon and tell me it smells like roses. I want his pecker in my pocket.*
Lyndon B. Johnson, on selecting a personal assistant

People said my language was bad but, Jesus, you should have heard LBJ!
Richard Nixon, 1913–1992, on Lyndon B. Johnson

Moving out of the English-speaking world, Napoleon Bonaparte, Napoleon I, Emperor of France, was a greatly feared general. He conquered most of Europe during his expansionist wars, before being defeated largely by a disastrous winter campaign in Russia. In contrast, Charles de Gaulle was the leader of the Free French, resisting Nazi forces during the Second World War. He resigned from politics, but was called back in the late 1950s to help during a national crisis; he re-wrote the constitution to allow for a president, and then took the position once he had created it. Economic recovery followed swiftly, so he was obiously doing something right. Despite the differences between the two men, both were inclined to bursts of insulting comment.

A pile of shit in a silk stocking.
Napoleon Bonaparte, 1769–1821, on Talleyrand

England is a nation of shopkeepers.
Napoleon Bonaparte, on the English

It is a matter of great interest what sovereigns are doing; but as to what Grand Duchesses are doing – who cares?
Napoleon Bonaparte, on the relative newsworthiness of the aristocracy.

When I am right, I get angry. Churchill gets angry when he is wrong. We are angry at each other much of the time.
Charles de Gaulle, 1890–1970, on Winston Churchill

Politics are too serious a matter to be left to the politicians.
Charles de Gaulle, on Clement Attlee

How can you govern a country which has 246 different varieties of cheese?
Charles de Gaulle, on France

If there is ever another war in Europe, it will come out of some damn silly thing in the Balkans.
Otto von Bismarck, uncannily predicting the cause of the First World War, too

If reactionary measures are to be carried, the Liberal Party takes the rudder, from the correct assumption that it will not overstep the necessary limits; if liberal measures are to be carried, the Conservative Party takes office in its turn for the same consideration.
Otto von Bismarck, on British politics

A lath of wood painted to look like iron.
Otto von Bismarck, on Lord Salisbury

That old Jew!
Otto von Bismarck, on Benjamin Disraeli

There is a providence that protects idiots, drunkards, children and the United States of America
Otto von Bismarck, on the USA's youthful exuberance and fortune

If the finest thinkers are a representation of the people at large, then the German national character must tend towards bitter, cynical resignation. From the Marxist playright Berthold Brecht to the more Darwinian philosopher Friedrich Nietzsche – who believed that absolute moral codes had no place in human life – the German populace have seemed less interested in politicians themselves than in the mess they leave behind.

The finest plans are always ruined by the littleness of those who ought to carry them out, for the Emperors can actually do nothing.
Berthold Brecht, 1898–1956, *Mother Courage*

One observes they have gone too long without a war here.
Berthold Brecht, Ibid.

War always finds a way.
Berthold Brecht, Ibid.

Don't tell me peace has broken out – I've just bought some new supplies.
Berthold Brecht, Ibid.

Andrea: Unhappy the land that has no heroes!
Galileo: No! Unhappy the land that needs heroes...
Berthold Brecht, *Life of Galileo*

Whenever I hear the word culture ... I release the safety catch of my Browning!
Hanns Johst, 1890–1978, on buzzwords

At the base of all these aristocratic races the predator is not to be mistaken, the splendorous blond beast, avidly rampant for plunder and victory.
Friedrich Nietzsche, 1844–1900, on governor as predator

In fact, moving beyond focused national borders and looking at the world as a whole – those sections of it whose politicians have been translated into English, anyway – quickly reveals that no matter what language you're talking in, and no matter which continent you are on, the politicians, commentators and critics are going to be snide about themselves, each other, their jobs, and pretty much everything else too. This is equally true of Europe...

Take away "Time is Money", and what is left of England? Take away "Cotton is King", and what is left of America?
Victor Hugo, 1802–1885, *Les Misérables*

Despotism accomplishes great things illegally; liberty doesn't even go to the trouble of accomplishing small things legally.
Honoré de Balzac, 1799–1850

God punish England!
Alfred Funke, 1869–1926, *Sword and Myrtle*

The majority never has right on its side. Never, I say! That is one of the social lies that a free, thinking man is bound to rebel against. Who makes up the majority in any given country? Is it the wise men or the fools? I think we must agree that the fools are in a terrible overwhelming majority, all the wide world over. But, damn it, it can surely never be right that the stupid should rule over the clever!
Henrik Ibsen, 1828–1906, *An Enemy of the People*

Written by Bible readers for Bible readers.
Jacques Bainville, 1879–1936, on the Treaty of Versailles

War is nothing but a continuation of politics with the admixture of other means.
Karl von Clausewitz, 1780–1831, *On War*

...Asia ...

The guilt of Stalin and his immediate entourage before the Party and the people for the mass repressions and lawlessness they committed is enormous and unforgivable.
Mikhail Gorbachev, 1931–

The atom bomb is a paper tiger which the United States reactionaries use to scare people. It looks terrible, but in fact it isn't. All reactionaries are paper tigers.
Mao Tse Tung, 1893–1976, engaging in a little propaganda

People of the world unite and defeat the US aggressors and all their running dogs!
Mao Tse Tung, on NATO and her allies

There is one eternally true legend – that of Judas.
Joseph Stalin, 1879–1953

A good man fallen among Fabians.
Lenin (Vladimir Ilyitch Ulianov), 1870–1924, on George Bernard Shaw

Of the best rulers, the people know only that they exist; the next best they love and praise; the next they fear; and the next they revile; but of the best, when their task is accomplished, their work done, the people all remark "We have done it ourselves".
Lao Tzu, *c.* 604–531BC

... the Americas ...

Those who have served the cause of the revolution have plowed the sea.
Simon Bolivar, 1783–1830, on Venezuela

The Falklands thing was a fight between two bald men over a comb.
Jorge Luis Borges, 1899–1986

Poor Mexico, so far from God and so close to the United States.
Porfirio Diaz, 1830–1915

... the African continent ...

History teaches us that men and nations behave wisely once they have exhausted all other alternatives.
Abba Eban, on life as an Israeli diplomat

A hotbed of cold feet.
Abba Eban, 1915–, on the British Foreign Office

Are you a politician who says to himself "I will use my country for my own benefit", or are you a devoted patriot who whispers in the ear of his inner self "I love to serve my country as a faithful servant"?
Kahlil Gibran, 1883–1931, *The New Frontier*, on Syrian politics

That would be a good idea.
Mahatma Gandhi, 1869–1948, when asked what he thought of modern civilization

Please go on. It is my day of silence.
Mahatma Gandhi, written on a note handed to a British representative at a meeting

My humanity is not dependent on the acceptance of white people.
Allan Boesak, 1945–, on losing an election in South Africa

... or Australasia. Although, everything considered, perhaps Australian politics is more robust in its insults than that of many other countries.

You look like an Easter Island statue with an arse full of razor blades.
Paul Keating, 1944–, to the Australian Prime Minister Malcolm Fraser

These are the same old fogies who doffed their lids and tugged the forelock to the British establishment.
Paul Keating, on Australian supporters of Great Britain

Even as it walked out on you and joined the Common Market, you were still looking for your MBEs and your knighthoods, and all the rest of the regalia that comes with it.
Paul Keating, on Great Britain and her Australian supporters

This little flower, this delicate little beauty, this cream puff, is supposed to be beyond personal criticism – he is simply a shiver looking for a spine to run up.
Paul Keating, on Australian Liberal leader John Hewson

I'm a bastard. But I'm a bastard who gets the mail delivered on time.
Paul Keating, on himself.

It wiggles, it's shapely and its name is Ainsley Gotto.
Dudley Erwin, 1917–1984, on the Australian Prime Minister's secretary, the "political manoeuvre" which supposedly ended his career.

Sometimes fiction is closer to reality than is commonly realized. The satirical political television series *Yes Minister* and its sequel *Yes Prime Minister* have been widely regarded as some of the most venomously lucid commentaries on the working of government and bureaucracy ever fictionalized. The central characters of Jim Hacker, a vain, cowardly and generally ignorant politician, and Sir Humphrey Appleby, his brilliant, obstructive and utterly mystifying bureaucratic aide, are considered two of the cruellest and most incisive stereotypes of the political system to date. The material is timeless, and exposes the dynamic ineptitude and inefficiency of what is commonly considered government – the perfect summary of political insults.

Opposition is about asking awkward questions, and government is about not answering them.
Jonathan Lynn (1943–) and Anthony Jay (1930–), *Yes Minister*

Ministers need activity. It's their substitute for achievement.
Ibid.

Years of political training and experience had taught him to use twenty words where one would do, to write millions of words where thousands would suffice, to use language to blur and fudge the issues and events so that they became incomprehensible to others. When incomprehensibility has been achieved by a politician, so has safety.
Ibid.

The Prime Minister, whose motto is ... "In defeat, malice – in victory, revenge!"
Ibid.

The Official Secrets Act is not to protect secrets but to protect officials.
Ibid.

Collective responsibility means that when we do something popular they all leak the fact that it was their idea, and when we do something unpopular they leak the fact that they were against it.
Jonathan Lynn and Anthony Jay, *Yes Prime Minister*, on the party's response to government actions

Diplomacy is about surviving till the next century. Politics is about surviving until Friday afternoon.
Ibid.

Step One: We must do something.
Step Two: This is something.
Step Three: Therefore we must do it.
Ibid., on the politician's three-step, action-packed response to any crisis

Popcorn is the last area of the movie business where good taste is still a concern.
The Oldie magazine on Hollywood, 1988

In surveys throughout the Western world, it has been shown that the public are more likely to recognize and know the names of famous film stars than their own political leaders. Legally speaking, the politicians have more power over us than entertainers, but the bulk of us pay far more attention to the stars than we do to the folks in suits who govern the country. Actors and actresses, musicians, artists and writers play a large part in shaping our attitudes and beliefs. Rich, famous, beautiful, they represent a tantalizing glimpse of the supposed golden life, something to fantasize about to relieve the boredom of normal working life.

From the outside peeking in, everything in movieland looks perfect. The rich and famous always talk about the huge despair of having wealth and privilege, but that's just to keep the rest of us off their backs, right? Maybe ... but maybe the golden life never existed, maybe it's all a big con, a media hype, to keep us interested. "If there's one thing worse than being talked about, it's not being talked about," said Oscar Wilde. We'll hear more from him later – quite a lot more – but here he hit the nail on the head. Whether people are being pleasant or unpleasant, fame is fame. People are fickle, and we have short memories and little loyalty towards our entertainers. That breeds rivalry, which in turns breeds jealousy, spite and malice – a bottomless spring pouring forth a broad torrent of insults.

In this section, we'll listen in on what the famous have to say about each other and, I'll warn you now, it isn't pretty. From the witty artistic circles of Victorian

England to the sets of Hollywood, there seem to be no depths to which some irate celebrity or other will not stoop in order to belittle a colleague. Much as they moan, though, almost none of the stars would be anywhere else, doing any other job. They're there to entertain us and, if that includes being catty about each other in public, we can only benefit. Other, sterner critics have cast aspersions on the entire field of professional entertainment:

I am persuaded that Satan has not a more speedy way and fitter school to work and teach his desire, to bring men and women in to share his filthy lusts of wicked whoredom than those plays and theatres.
John Northbrooke, 1542–1608

One should never take one's daughter to a theatre. Not only are the plays immoral; the house itself is immoral.
Alexandre Dumas, 1824–1895

Sinful, heathenish, lewd, ungodly spectacles, and most pernicious corruptions; condemned in all ages as intolerable mischiefs to churches, to republics, to the manners, minds and souls of men. The profession of play-poets, of stage-players, together with the penning, acting and frequenting of stage-plays, are unlawful, infamous and misbeseeming Christians.
William Prynne, 1600–1669

Aside from the moral contamination incident to the average theatre, the influence intellectually is degrading. Its lessons are morbid, distorted, and superficial; they do not mirror life.
T.T. Munger, 1827–1904

There is a total extinction of all taste: our authors are vulgar, gross, illiberal; the theatre swarms with wretched translations and ballad operas, and we have nothing new but improving abuse.
Horace Walpole, 1717–1797

Others have been more specific with their disapproval. Here, it's not so much that the field of entertainment itself is reprehensible – just certain segments of it.

You can pick out the actors by the glazed look that comes into their eyes when the conversation wanders away from themselves.
Michael Wilding, 1912–1979

Some of the greatest love affairs I've known have involved one actor, unassisted.
Wilson Mizner, 1876 –1933

That's a lot of money to see buggers jump.
Nigel Bruce, 1895–1953, on the cost of ballet

Is it a stale remark to say that I have constantly found the interest excited at a playhouse to bear an exact inverse proportion to the price paid for admission?
Charles Lamb, 1775–1834

Musicals: a series of catastrophes ending with a floorshow.
Oscar Levant, 1906–1972

Fame is, in many ways, the ultimate expression of the hopes and dreams that most of us have. It is the pinnacle of our desires: power and wealth without responsibility or drudgery ... a very tempting proposition. Nowhere is that influence stronger than in Hollywood. It is the heart of the film industry – in fact, for many people, it *is* the film industry – and the movies themselves are the heart of entertainment. The very name conjures up images of glitz, glamour, high-powered parties and wild, unbridled nights. What we forget, those of us who are not part of that image, is that we are talking about the place where illusions are made. Movies are organized deception – none of what we see on the screens is real – so is it any surprise to find out that perhaps the image of the place itself is also a deception? There are certainly plenty of stars who think this is the case, and they'd know...

Strip the phoney tinsel off Hollywood and you'll find the real tinsel underneath.
Oscar Levant

Hollywood is a place where people from Iowa mistake each other for stars.
Fred Allen, 1894–1956

I've spent several years in Hollywood, and I still think the movie heroes are in the audience.
Wilson Mizner

A leader of public thought in Hollywood wouldn't have sufficient mental acumen anywhere else to hold down a place in the bread line.
Anita Loos, 1893–1981

Hollywood impresses me as being ten million dollars' worth of intricate and highly ingenious machinery functioning elaborately to put the skin on baloney.
George Jean Nathan, 1882–1958

Hollywood buys a good story about a bad girl and changes it to a bad story about a good girl.
Anon.

The only "ism" Hollywood believes in is plagiarism.
Dorothy Parker, 1893–1967

God felt sorry for actors, so he created Hollywood to give them a place in the sun and a swimming pool. The price they had to pay was to surrender their talent.
Cedric Hardwicke, 1893–1964

Life in Hollywood can actually be brutally unpleasant. For the thousands of near-broke – or soon-to-be near-broke, as there are many predators – hopefuls who arrive every day from all over the world desperately hoping somehow to make it, life is often really rather horrendous. But even the fortunate few, the stars, often find that the Hollywood life isn't everything it's cracked up to be.

Hollywood is a carnival where there are no concessions ... a sewer, with service from the Ritz Carlton.
Wilson Mizner

In Hollywood, if you don't have happiness, you send out for it.
Rex Reed, 1938–

In Hollywood, all the marriages are happy – it's trying to live together afterwards that causes the problems.
Shelley Winters, 1922–

Hollywood is a great place if you're an orange.
Fred Allen

The title "Little Napoleon" in Hollywood is equivalent to the title "Mister" in any other community.
Alva Johnston, 1888–1950

The frantic pace of life at the top has always produced a fascinating range of offensive behaviour. Although many actors and actresses are rumoured to be a little light on intellectual ability, plenty of them have also been blessed with a lightning-fast wit. There are a few stars whose names are unavoidably linked with rapier-like put-downs, and one of the mightiest of them is Groucho Marx. Actually named Julius, Groucho got his nickname from his bad temper. Always appearing with his characteristic thick black eyebrows and moustache, a big cigar and a funny walk, he was so distinctive that 20 years after his death his caricature is instantly recognizable. He was a master of insults, bitterly funny, and definitely not someone to cross verbal swords with.

From the moment I picked your book up until I put it down, I was convulsed with laughter. Some day I intend reading it.
Groucho Marx, 1890–1977

I never forget a face – but in your case, I'll be glad to make an exception.
Groucho Marx

I've had a wonderful evening, but this wasn't it.
Groucho Marx

Please accept my resignation. I don't want to belong to any club that will accept me as a member.
Groucho Marx

She got her good looks from her father – he's a plastic surgeon.
Groucho Marx

Oh, sorry, I thought you were a fellow I knew.
Groucho Marx to Greta Garbo, after she ignored a friendly "Hello"

I never like a movie where the hero's tits are bigger than the heroine's.
Groucho Marx, on *Samson & Delilah*, starring Victor Mature and Hedy Lamarr

I knew her before she was a virgin.
Groucho Marx, on Doris Day

The man was a major comedian, which is to say that he had the compassion of an icicle, the effrontery of a carnival shill, and the generosity of a pawnbroker.
S.J. Perelman, 1904–1979, on Groucho Marx

Another ferocious verbal opponent was Bette Davis. Known as difficult to be with – both on and off set – she was imperious, judgmental and outspoken. She never stinted herself when it came to criticizing others, and gained a reputation for being altogether terrifying. Her screen presence was distinctive. She spoke with a very precise voice, and used cigarettes to great effect. She generally played forceful, independent women, appropriately enough. Reputed to be a voracious sexual predator, she had four marriages and dozens of affairs, which included several high-profile lovers, such as the eccentric millionaire Howard Hughes. With good looks, talent, success, fame and wealth come enemies, and many of Bette's most cutting outbursts were directed at her female rivals within the movie industry. She was particularly scornful of Joan Crawford, due to certain old sexual disagreements.

I wouldn't sit on her toilet.
Bette Davis, 1908–1989, on Joan Crawford

Hollywood's first case of syphilis.
Bette Davis, on Joan Crawford

One area of life Joan should never have gotten into was children. She bought them...
Bette Davis, on Joan Crawford

She was a swine!
Bette Davis, on Miriam Hopkins

Faye Dunaway is the most unprofessional actress I ever worked with, and that includes Miriam Hopkins, even.
Bette Davis, on Faye Dunaway

She's the original good time that was had by all.
Bette Davis, on Marilyn Monroe

After The Wizard of Oz, *Constance Bennett was known as the Wicked Witch of the West. A witch on heels, if you want to be polite. Although she was very highly paid at one time, she represented the sort of actress for whom I had contempt – the type that cared more about makeup than motivation. Her face was her talent, and when it dropped, so did her career, right out of sight.*
Bette Davis, on Constance Bennett

I watched Barbara Stanwyck in The Thorn Birds. *Augh! It was painful!*
Bette Davis, on Barbara Stanwyck

It's a very good play, but I told Beryl Reid, the actress who starred in it, that she had to star in the movie version. And she did. That role was absolutely her.
Bette Davis, on turning down a lesbian role in *The Killing of Sister George*

You were very good, Olivia. When you weren't in a scene with me, you managed to keep the audience's attention.
Bette Davis, to Olivia de Havilland

Nowadays, the women are all sexually aggressive to an extreme, like Madonna, and the men are sexually passive or not at all, like Michael Jackson. Worst of all, the biggest stars in Hollywood aren't even actors; they're singers whose voices are undistinguished and merely serviceable.
Bette Davis, on the modern film industry

It would be a dreadful mistake to think that Davis reserved all her ire for other women, though. There were plenty of men who fell foul of her acid humour.

This is an actor who plays by himself to himself. In this particular picture he plays a dual role, so at least he was able to play with himself.
Bette Davis, on Alec Guinness in *The Scapegoat*

He needed willowy or boyish girls like Katherine Hepburn to make him look what they now call macho. If I'd co-starred with Grant or if Crawford had, we'd have eaten him for breakfast!
Bette Davis, on Cary Grant

I never worked with him, but I had a brief crush on Gable. One day, I happened to mention it to my dentist, in his office. I was fairly new to Los Angeles, but a few dentists serviced most of the stars. This one was also Gable's dentist, and he asked what I particularly liked about Gable. I said, "His bright smile." He said, "Would you like to see that bright smile today?" My heart was pounding. I thought Gable must be the next patient, after me. I could hardly wait for the session to end, and then the dentist led me to an adjoining room and there, under glass, was a pair of Gable's very white dentures...
Bette Davis, on Clark Gable

Gary Merrill was a macho man, but none of my four husbands was man enough to become Mr Bette Davis.
Bette Davis, on marriage and her fourth husband

We had tremendous fights. He used his fists more than his mouth. It was a hell of a marriage, even the making up. They ought to rewrite the ceremony – "in sickness and in hell".
Bette Davis, on Gary Merrill

Dick Cavett thinks he's TV's brightest, funniest star. What ever gave him that idea? He's far from the funniest, just the shortest.
Bette Davis, on Dick Cavett

Unsurprisingly, there were legions of dedicated foes always waiting to take a stab back at Bette. It seems to be one of the natural laws of the universe that anyone outspoken and uncomplimentary will tend to attract criticism.

After all the nice things I've said about that hag! When I get hold of her, I'll tear every hair out of her moustache!
Tallulah Bankhead, 1903–1968, irritated by Bette Davis

I saw Bette in a hotel in Madrid once and went up to her and said, "Miss Davis, I'm Ava Gardner and I'm a great fan of yours." She behaved exactly as I wanted her to behave. "Of course you are, my dear," she said, "of course you are." And then she swept on.
Ava Gardner, 1922–1990, on Bette Davis

I was at a restaurant, and there was Bette Davis. She didn't look as if she were enjoying her lunch. In fact, she was harassing the help and carrying on, and she didn't let up until the moment she left. It was quite disillusioning, because I'd thought Miss Davis was a great actress – I found out she wasn't acting on the screen; she was just being her ornery self!
Vera-Ellen, 1926–1981, on Bette Davis

She should have played my grandmother, not my mother.
Susan Hayward, 1918–1975, on working with Bette Davis

I don't hate Bette Davis, even though the press wants me to. I resent her – I don't see how she built a career out of a set of mannerisms instead of acting ability. Take away the pop eyes, the cigarette and those funny clipped words and what have you got? She's a phoney, but I guess the public likes that.
Joan Crawford, 1906–1977, on Bette Davis

Working with Bette was one of the greatest challenges I've ever had ... Bette is of a different temperament than I. She has to yell every morning. I just sat and knitted. I knitted a scarf from Hollywood to Malibu.
Joan Crawford, on Bette Davis

A controversial actress, Joan Crawford had a reputation for being quite a bitch in her private life. She used to draw up timetables planning out her third husband's days, and she was constantly followed by quiet murmurs about her ill-treatment of her adopted children. She was known to have made several pornographic movie reels during her early career – including, most famously, an explicit film ironically titled *Casting Couch* – and one collector of this early material died in a fire some weeks after refusing to sell certain pictures to her. Like her foe Bette Davis, Crawford was sexually voracious. She often shocked friends and acquaintances with both her tongue and her clothes; they never quite knew what to expect from the flamboyant, eccentric star.

Her delight was to create friction. "Did you hear what he said about you?" she'd tell me. "And in front of a group of people!"... I was as civil as I knew how to be.
Joan Crawford, on Mercedes McCambridge

In the 1930s, bosoms came back in again, so I was in luck, but Carole required some artificial help. Before she would go before the cameras, she was famous for yelling out to her costumers, "Bring me my breasts!"
Joan Crawford, on Carole Lombard

It's sad that today's actresses feel they have to resort to advertising to make extra money. Esther Williams is selling swimwear and Marilyn Monroe sells everything under the sun. I don't mean that unkindly, but in my day, actresses had more class than that.
Joan Crawford, plainly forgetting her hat-selling days...

I like to think every director I've worked with has fallen a little in love with me. I know Dorothy Arzner did.
Joan Crawford, on Dorothy Arzner

I was married to the brother of St Nick. You know that picture Miracle on 34th Street? *The one who played Santa Claus – I forget his name. Anyway, his brother – that's who I was married to. I forget his name as well...*
Estelle Winwood, on marriage to Arthur Chesney, Edmund Gwenn's brother

I did have one homosexual husband. At least. Guthrie McClintic. He was an extremely famous Broadway producer who loved his fellow man – often. I wasn't the only actress he married. He married Katherine Cornell. But it was different for her than it was for me – like her husband, she was attracted to her own kind. You know: Birds of a feather fornicate together.
Estelle Winwood, on Guthrie McClintic

The last time I saw her, she snubbed me. Cut me dead. I said so to a friend of mine, who said it must have been because I stayed thin...
Estelle Winwood, on Hermione Gingold

One day, during a dress rehearsal, during the break, she wailed at me, wringing her hands "Oh, where-oh-where would I be without Alfred?" I decided to tell her, because she wasn't getting any younger. I said "You'd be right here, where I am, playing your mother."
Estelle Winwood, on Lynn Fontanne and Alfred Lunt

Mr Shaw was born old... He was rumoured to be neutral about sex... Shaw would have made a perfect priest, except he happened to be an atheist.
Estelle Winwood, on George Bernard Shaw

Funny about both Margaret Rutherford and Margaret Hamilton. Both were dreadfully plain in their youth. The older they got, the easier they were to look at... Time does heal some wounds.
Estelle Winwood, on the effects of age

The first major star to announce publicly that he had AIDS, Rock Hudson started off as a truck driver. His good looks got him into the cinema – he had no acting experience whatsoever when he started out, and later on in his career he had to have intensive coaching. He hid his homosexuality throughout most of his time as an actor, and the announcement of his disease shocked the world. No stranger to diatribe and verbal assault, Hudson was skilled at putting people in their place. He reserved the majority of his bitchiness for his female colleagues.

Doris Day was not only the eternal virgin, she was the eternal Pollyanna! She didn't care for reality or for people all that much, and she found her ideal philosophy and atmosphere in Christian Science and in dogs. She as much as informed the press that she loved her dogs more than she loved her only child.
Rock Hudson, 1925–1985, on Doris Day

I tell you the truth. I wouldn't even stand next to her at a cocktail party.
Rock Hudson, on Susan Saint James

Jane Wyman has had the same girlish hairdo for decades ... but she's not a girl any more, and it's starting to look a little grisly...
Rock Hudson, on Jane Wyman

I heard that my Darling Lily *taskmasters, Blake Edwards and Julie Andrews, were implying to the press that I'm gay. I could hardly believe it! Talk about the kettle calling the pot black!*
Rock Hudson, on Julie Andrews and Blake Edwards

I'm in love with Julie Andrews, yes. There's nothing I wouldn't say to her face – both of them.
Rock Hudson, on Julie Andrews

Lily Tomlin has been in and out of the closet more times than my hunting jacket.
Rock Hudson, on Lily Tomlin's sexual privacy

Why is it that the wildest personal rumours accrue to the most innocuous actresses? There's the rumour that June Allyson is an alleged nymphomaniac and the one that Julie Andrews is tougher than a five-star general.
Rock Hudson, on the Hollywood gossip mill

Hudson was perfectly prepared to be rude about the men in his immediate vicinity too, of course.

I did not give Lee Majors his start in acting. You can't pin that one on me. Technically, he hasn't started acting yet. He had a pretty face, then he got a pretty wife, now he has a pretty career.
Rock Hudson, on Lee Majors

I did a movie with the Duke and was very surprised to find out that he had small feet, wore lifts and a corset. Hollywood is seldom what it seems...
Rock Hudson, on John Wayne

Paul is a little paunchy, even though he doesn't eat desserts. Popcorn's his dessert – one of them...
Rock Hudson, on Paul Newman

An old queen from way, way back ... As the New York Times *would say, "A confirmed bachelor".*
Rock Hudson, on Billy De Wolfe

Given the stresses associated with keeping a large section of a public life strictly private, Hudson inevitably attracted much criticism. Repressed by public opinion – he even married his agent's secretary for a while – and somewhat personally neurotic, he alienated a variety of people, for a variety of reasons.

He was a shallow little boy who may have grown tall but never grew up. Self-centred and spoiled, he could never communicate on any level that did not relate to himself.
Martha Hyer, 1924–, on Rock Hudson

Rock Hudson was emotionally constipated. He hated having to play hetero on screen, he hated having to pretend off-screen, and he hated anyone saying he was gay. We acted together, but we could never have socialized. I let it all hang out; he left it all hanging in. Now that he's not a big star anymore, he's still just as uptight!
Paul Lynde, 1926–1982, on Rock Hudson

I knew right away that Rock Hudson was gay when he did not fall in love with me.
Gina Lollobrigida, 1927–, on Rock Hudson

Rock Hudson surrounded himself with fellow closet queens, horrible, selfish, self-loathing older men. The day after Rock died of AIDS, one of them went on national TV to say that Rock had died of anorexia, and another went on TV to deny that Rock was gay! This was all by way of saving their own silly skins, staying in that closet forever...
Peter Allen, 1944–1992, on Rock Hudson

A miserable newspaper woman wrote something implying that Rock Hudson, Julie and I were a sexual threesome. She also implied that Rock and I had spent a lot of time together in San Francisco leather bars. I walked up to Rock and repeated the story to him, and I loved his response: "How in the hell did she find out so quick?"
Blake Edwards, 1922–, on Rock Hudson and Julie Andrews

Flamboyant and self-accepting in a way that Hudson never managed to emulate, writer and journalist Truman Capote was a regular member of the Hollywood scene. The author of *Breakfast At Tiffany's* was no stranger to scandal – in fact, his last book, published after his death, was a novel of socialite gossip. Colourful, wicked and at times very funny, Capote had a sharp tongue which he was prepared to wield against all manner of prominent targets.

Anthony Perkins is awful, I can't stand him. There's nothing there, and he pretends not to know if he's really gay or not. Just ask any one of the small army of his ex-lovers! Of which I am not one! I don't like blood, and Tony's a sadist. He likes to see blood. I mean, he is Norman Bates!
Truman Capote, 1924–1984, on Anthony Perkins

McCarthy says he had no idea that Monty Clift was homosexual and was absolutely amazed. Why, he said, it never even crossed his mind. Well, it had crossed the mind of every single trolley-car conductor in Hollywood, so it was very difficult to believe it hadn't crossed the mind of his best friend for seven and a half years. I mean, how far can hypocrisy go?
Truman Capote, on Monty Clift and Kevin McCarthy

Rod Steiger's the worst actor that ever lived. The very name makes me throw up. He's so terrible. He's one of the world's worst hams. A real jambon!
Truman Capote, on Rod Steiger

Brando told me that Jimmy used to call him on the phone all the time, and Marlon would listen to him talking to the answering service, and he wouldn't answer, wouldn't speak up. This was just one of the more disgusting aspects of Marlon's.
Truman Capote, on Marlon Brando and James Dean

I am not a fan of Meryl Streep. Or, as I call her, Meryl Creep. I think she's creepy. Anyway, life is difficult enough without Meryl Streep movies.
Truman Capote, on Meryl Streep

She looks like a truck driver in drag.
Truman Capote, on Jacqueline Susann

Capote was actually sued by Jacqueline Susann for a million dollars over the above slight. However, as he gleefully recounted, she was advised to drop the case before it got to court, because if the defence had brought a range of truck drivers in for comparison she'd probably have lost... Unlike many of the film stars, Capote also turned his gaze on Hollywood life, not just on the people around him.

He was mean as hell to her, and they lived right next door to me, for years. He would holler and get terribly angry, and she would take refuge in my apartment. She would hide, and Johnny would come pounding on my door, shouting "I know she's in there." I would just maintain a dead silence.
Truman Capote, on Johnny Carson and his second wife, Joanne

Most short men are sort of insecure. Look at Dick Cavett. But Nick Adams had a lifelong love affair with himself. Of course, that's not difficult when you're gay.
Truman Capote, on height

They can ruin your book in two ways... They cast Audrey Hepburn in my Breakfast At Tiffany's, *and I adore Audrey, but she was miscast – she is no hillbilly! Nor, really, a tomboy. Jodie Foster would be ideal in a remake... But worst of all, they chose a horrible director, Blake Edwards, who I could spit on! And they cast Mickey Rooney as a Japanese – I just wanted to throw up!*
Truman Capote, on his disappointment with the filming of *Breakfast At Tiffany's*

Capote was also perfectly happy to be outspoken outside of Tinseltown. He was critical of entertainers in other fields – such as literature, music and politics:

Gore Vidal has never written a novel that's readable, with the exception of Myra Breckenridge, *which you can sort of thumb your way through. His novels are unbelievably bad.*
Truman Capote, on Gore Vidal

On The Road – *that's not writing, that's typing.*
Truman Capote, on Jack Kerouac's magnum opus

I'm surprised none of the Kennedys have gone into show business. We have mediocre actors becoming politicians, but we never seem to have politicians turning their deceptive skills to the silver screen. I guess the only fictitious characters they like to portray are themselves.
Truman Capote, on the Kennedy dynasty

She takes every ballad and turns it into a three-act opera. She simply cannot leave a song alone!
Truman Capote, on Barbra Streisand

I couldn't stand her. The Jap. She was always paranoid. The most unpleasant person that ever was, in my opinion. She's a bore.
Truman Capote, on Yoko Ono

Fellow writer Gore Vidal was always prepared to return Capote's criticism as maliciously as possible, not that he was the only one.

A republican housewife from Kansas with all the prejudices
Gore Vidal, 1925–, on Truman Capote

Truman Capote has made lying an art. A minor art.
Gore Vidal, on Truman Capote

Liberace and Capote – I never can get those two straight.
Milton Berle, 1908–, on Truman Capote

Often dismissed as a dizzy redhead, Lucille Ball was actually a razor-sharp comedienne with a great deal of showbiz acumen. A brilliant innovator in the television industry, she set in place a great many sitcom elements that we take for granted nowadays. With her husband Desi Arnaz, a Cuban bandleader, she developed the three-camera filming technique for shooting programmes being recorded live, and *I Love Lucy* was in fact the first sitcom to be filmed in front of an audience. She also came up with the idea of syndicated TV programmes. Her shows are still broadcast in many countries. Along with her undeniable skill, she also had a fiery temper and a cutting way with words.

Didn't Orson Welles look porcine to you? I don't mean his weight, necessarily. His face – he had a piggy-looking face ... something around the nostrils. I always thought that if they filmed George Orwell's Animal Farm *with human actors, Orson could play the head pig who took over the farm.*
Lucille Ball, 1911–1989, on Orson Welles

Orson Welles should have played in The Man Who Came To Dinner. *As a houseguest, he was a nightmare! He completely took over the house, no request or demand was too big for him to make, and he sincerely believed he was bestowing a blessing by his very presence.*
Lucille Ball, on Orson Welles

I'm not going to repeat any rumours I've heard, but on the screen she almost never played a woman...
Lucille Ball, on Eve Arden

Desi is a loser. A gambler, an alcoholic, a skirt-chaser ... a financially smart man, but self-destructive. He's just a loser.
Lucille Ball, on Desi Arnaz

Lucy isn't a redhead for no reason. She has a big comic talent, but she also has a big, not very funny temper. Not a temperament, but a temper. Her tongue is a lethal weapon.
Desi Arnaz, 1917–1986, on Lucille Ball

Lucille Ball was a control freak. Had to be in charge of everything.
Phyllis Diller, 1917–, on Lucille Ball

Extravagant, wild, seductive ... Tallulah Bankhead was untamed, an unusual experience in many different ways. Chain-smoking and chain-drinking, with a deep, throaty voice and a fondness for shocking people, she was famous for her exhibitionism. At other people's parties, she would often take her clothes off and socialize naked; parties she threw herself tended to last – literally – for days, and guests would bring pyjamas. She covered up her appalling memory for names by calling everyone "dahling", which became something of a personal trademark. Her wit was as infamous as her temper, but it had an unusual genesis; she got muddled in conversation with renowned theatre critic Alexander Woolcott, who had invited the young, inexperienced actress to an opening night, and turned a bland compliment into a devastating insult, shown below. Woolcott quoted her in his column the following day, and a legend was born.

There's less to this play than meets the eye...
Tallulah Bankhead, 1903–1968, to Alexander Woolcott

The biggest phoney in Hollywood, dahling! A lying lesbo, a Polish publicity hound! She showed up at Valentino's funeral and pretended they'd fallen in love and been engaged to be married – didn't leave her a cent, dahling! To

demonstrate her grief for the cameras, she fainted at the funeral, not just once, but on request. A lousy actress. Had a moustache and couldn't act her way out of a paper bag!
Tallulah Bankhead, on Pola Negri

Dietrich? She's okay if you like cheekbones, dahling.
Tallulah Bankhead, on Marlene Dietrich.

How the hell should I know, dahling? He never sucked my *cock!*
Tallulah Bankhead, when asked about Tab Hunter's rumoured homosexuality

No, I cannot accept that Lynn Fontanne is what some theatregoers call a diva. She is half of a team, and as she always acts with her husband, who knows if she alone can carry a play or if she would have as many, or half as many, loyal fans on her own?
Tallulah Bankhead, on Lynn Fontanne

Bankhead left plenty of tales behind her, but fewer enemies. Although there are many actresses who would consider the quotes below to be deadly insults, Tallulah would undoubtedly have laughed uproariously at them, and added a few choice comments of her own.

I remember Tallulah telling of going into a public ladies' room and discovering there was no toilet tissue. She looked underneath the booth and said to the lady in the next stall, "I beg your pardon, do you happen to have any toilet tissue in there?" The lady said no. So Tallulah said, "Well then, dahling, do you have two fives for a ten?"
Ethel Merman, 1904–1984, on Tallulah Bankhead

I did a movie with Miss Bankhead in England. One day, she wandered into my dressing room completely nude. I couldn't help staring, and she said "What's the matter, dahling? Haven't you ever seen a

blonde before?"
Donald Sutherland, 1934–, on Tallulah Bankhead

I was in Hitchcock's Lifeboat. *So was Tallulah Bankhead, who didn't wear panties, and each morning when we climbed into a lifeboat – up on a mechanical rocker – she gave the cast and crew a hell of a view, hiking up her skirt! Eventually someone complained to Hitch, who didn't want to get involved. He explained that it was an interdepartmental matter – involving wardrobe, costume, and possibly hairdressing...*
Hume Cronyn, 1911–, on Tallulah Bankhead

Alcohol does things to your face and skin. You don't get away scott free. Pretence is futile. Look at Tallulah Bankhead. Or me.
Geraldine Page, 1924–1987, on Tallulah Bankhead

Estelle Winwood is not Tallulah's best friend! I am! And I've got the scars to prove it!
Patsy Kelly, 1910–1981, on Tallulah Bankhead

Tallulah had more girlfriends than Errol Flynn!
Patsy Kelly, on Tallulah Bankhead

Tallulah never beat about the bush – she'd gossip about you in front of your back!
Patsy Kelly, on Tallulah Bankhead

A day away from Tallulah is like a month in the country.
Show Business Illustrated magazine, 1946, on Tallulah Bankhead

She is always skating on thin ice, and the British public wants to be there when it breaks.
Beatrice Stella Campbell, 1865–1940, on Tallulah Bankhead

More of an act than an actress.
Anonymous, on Tallulah Bankhead

Tallulah Bankhead is a marvellous female impersonator.
Anne Baxter, 1923–1985, on Tallulah Bankhead

Elsa Lanchester was a delicate English actress with a tongue like a file. Most famous for playing the title role in *The Bride of Frankenstein*, she was married to actor Charles Laughton from 1929 until his death in the early 1960s. Several critics felt that she could have had a higher profile if she had not been attached to Laughton. Her acidic comments made many people uneasy, particularly coming as they did from such a beautiful woman.

She's better on stage, from a distance. On a screen, up close, she makes you want to dive for cover.
Elsa Lanchester, 1902–1986, on Maggie Smith

I respect and admire Estelle Winwood; after all, she's so old, you almost have to. I think it's so quaint that she's making a whole new career out of merely being very old. But I hope I never live so long that I get hired simply for not being a corpse!
Elsa Lanchester, on Estelle Winwood

Patty Duke's behaviour during Me, Natalie *was most erratic. I didn't know what to make of it. I thought she was a Method actress. Afterwards someone informed me she was merely a manic-depressive.*
Elsa Lanchester, on Patty Duke

No-one remembers that she flirted with everyone, both sexes alike. I was a mere slip of a girl at the time, but she made a pass at me. I was sophisticated enough to recognize it for what it was, but young enough to decline...
Elsa Lanchester, on Isadora Duncan

Isadora was by no means a lithe or lovely woman. She was plump and "handsome".
Elsa Lanchester, on Isadora Duncan

I tried to like Miss Young, but she didn't make it easy, pretending to be so wholly holy all the time. Her one big flaw is her two faces.
Elsa Lanchester, on Loretta Young

Charles Laughton was not handsome. But I resented it when people called me "the bride of Frankenstein" behind my back – Charles did not appear in my most famous film.
Elsa Lanchester, on Charles Laughton and her role in *The Bride of Frankenstein*

For years, Miss Davis has been quoting a piece of advice she says Charles gave her: "Never dare not to hang yourself." It sounds like Charles, but I've yet to see evidence that he or Miss Davis has acted on it... Something to look forward to, I suppose.
Elsa Lanchester, on Bette Davis and Charles Laughton

Lanchester's humour may have been daunting, but not so much that there weren't people prepared to be critical of her.

Poor Elsa. She left England because it already had a queen – Victoria – and she wanted to be queen of the Charles Laughton household, once he became a star, but he already had the role.
Marlene Dietrich, 1901–1992, on Elsa Lanchester and Charles Laughton

She chose to hide her bushel under Charles Laughton's great big light...
Hermione Gingold, 1897–1987, on Elsa Lanchester

Elsa Lanchester is to Englishwomen what Madame Defarge is to Frenchwomen. Only England doesn't have the guillotine ... and Elsa uses her tongue to slice.
Hermione Baddeley, 1906–1986, on Elsa Lanchester

A child actress – she was in *Miracle on 34th Street* at the age of 9 – Natalie Wood progressed naturally into the Hollywood limelight when she got older. Despite criticism that she couldn't really act, she remained popular with the fans. She was married to actor Robert Wagner, and drowned in her early forties. Her insults and put-downs tended to be less vitriolic than those many other stars indulged in.

When we met and I was going to compliment her on her Oscar for Who's Afraid of Virginia Woolf?, *she did more talking than I did. I could hardly get a word in.*
Natalie Wood, 1938–1981, on Sandy Dennis

A director who used to be a writer isn't much use very often. A writer-director is worse.
Natalie Wood, on directors

I asked Bette Davis if she'd ever wanted to meet the Queen. She snapped at me, "What for? I am a queen." I wasn't going to argue with her!
Natalie Wood, on Bette Davis

He can relate to what actors have to go through. Plus, he had the sense to make a smart career change! If I were a lousy star, I'd certainly try and find something else...
Natalie Wood, on actor-turned-director Sydney Pollack

Natalie Wood will be sensational in Gypsy. *She plays a stripper.*
Rosalind Russell, 1908–1976, on Natalie Wood

Natalie Wood played Maria, the Puerto Rican damsel in West Side Story. *Natalie lost.*
Leonard Bernstein, 1918–1995, on Natalie Wood

I used to think Elvis Presley seemed unwholesome – as did much of the public. But he looks like a choirboy next to this singer they call Prince. I don't agree that Elvis Presley is the king of rock and roll, but if he were Prince would be the toadstool.
James Mason, on the artist formerly known as Prince

I pronounce it Charlotte Tramp-ling, and nobody ever notices I'm describing the role she always plays.
James Mason, on Charlotte Rampling

Mayer treated Judy abominably. She was the lowest-paid star in The Wizard of Oz. *Only Toto got paid less.*
James Mason, on Louis B. Mayer and Judy Garland

Merle went Hollywood before she went to Hollywood. She would do anything and everything to become a star. That included passing off her own mother, who was from India, as her maid... Then she went to Hollywood and she left her Jewish husband and married a cameraman so she could look beautiful via an interested expert, because her half-Indian complexion caused her great difficulties on screen. Of course by the time she arrived in Hollywood, her mother had died and been buried in an unmarked grave, part of Merle's hidden, secret past.
James Mason, on Merle Oberon

Dudley Moore has a club foot. That's not a problem – for him, his career, or anyone. What I object to is his club wit. Have you ever been chatted up by him at a cocktail party?
James Mason, on Dudley Moore

He was like a eunuch. For one thing, he was a voyeur. Terrified of sex but dying to watch or peep. He was fat and squishy and the most asexual man I've ever known.
James Mason, on Alfred Hitchcock

Another popular British actor in Hollywood, David Niven also had a broad mean streak in his verbal arsenal. Famed for his polished appearance and his military bearing, he was a genuine soldier. He attended Sandhurst military academy, and served for two years in Malta. When the Second World War started he was a major film star, but he re-entered the army as part of the rifle brigade and served throughout the war. When he returned to Hollywood, the Lieutenant Colonel was awarded the Order of Merit by General Eisenhower. He had a good sense of humour, and his two autobiographical books were best-sellers. He had little patience for fools...

She was doing a scene, urging Richard the Lionheart to go to the Middle East and fight. Loretta read her line, "Richard, you gotta save Christianity!", but not very convincingly. So DeMille took her aside and asked her to put some awe into her line reading. They reshot the scene, and she said "Aw, Richard, you gotta save Christianity!"
David Niven, 1909–1983, on Loretta Young

Miss United Dairies herself.
David Niven, on Jayne Mansfield

Some years after we worked together, he asked me why Hollywood had virtually ignored him – England too. I really couldn't answer the man. How could I tell him that he's only funny in Spanish?
David Niven, on Cantinflas, "the Mexican Chaplin"

There were prima donnas in the old days as well. I worked with Orson Welles... By that point, I think Welles had ceased caring about art and settled into a celebrity attitude.
David Niven, on Orson Welles

The scuttlebutt that was Virginia Valli was more butch than Charles Farrell, ditto Mary Livingstone vis-á-vis Jack Benny. More than a few of your celebrated actor-actress marriages aren't entirely what they seem...
David Niven, on sexuality in marriage

Did you know Dolores Del Rio's first two husbands were queer? The first was a Mexican. He shot himself. The second was MGM's self-inflated art director Cedric Gibbons. I never did get around to asking her why she never had children. Or whether she wanted any.
David Niven, on Dolores Del Rio

We are privileged to see Mr Samuel Goldwyn's latest "discovery". All we can say about this actor is that he is tall, dark, and not the slightest bit handsome.
Detroit Free Press, on David Niven

Although the art of the creative insult is one that has been stifled in modern years – litigation is a favourite past-time in the Western world, and being bitchy in public is one sure way to find yourself in court – it is good to know that today's stars are still being unpleasant about each other in a wide variety of ways. Maybe the bad old days of vitriol have passed, at least for the moment, but the spotlight of stardom still works nicely as a targeting aid for all the mud that's being slung.

It was a fabulous evening, and over dinner he admitted to me that he had always wanted to be Judy Garland, and that's God's honest truth.
Elton John, 1947–, on David Bowie

Working with Barbra Streisand is pretty stressful. It's like sitting down to a picnic in the middle of a freeway.
Kris Kristofferson, 1936–, on Barbra Streisand

Kevin Costner... I call him "personality-minus".
Frankie Howerd, 1922–1992, on Kevin Costner

Harry Cohn was an A1 stinker. Nickname: Genghis Cohn. He once interviewed me, with an eye towards hiring me. As you may know, I lost my right eye at the age of three, and he wouldn't come out and say it – he kept referring to my "deficiency". I thought he meant vitamins or something. Then he tells me I'm off-center on my vision and it'll show on the screen. So I do a screen test to prove that it doesn't, and he calls me back into his office and explains "Thank you Mr Falk, but for the same money I can get an actor with two eyes."
Peter Falk, 1927–, on Harry Cohn

You can't go around getting flowers from a fag like that!
André Agassi, 1970–, to Pete Sampras, on Elton John

If David Bowie's latest persona is the Thin White Duke, *he's going to give a bad name to whites, thin people and peers of the realm.*
Freddie Mercury, 1946–1991, on David Bowie

Is he just doing a bad Elvis pout, or was he born that way?
Freddie Mercury, on Billy Idol's sneer

Whatever happened to John Travolta? I heard he joined some cult and got fat. Or he married and had a child. Which amounts to the same thing.
Gérard Depardieu, 1948–, on John Travolta

Bruce Lee was an egomaniac. He thought it was terrible that he had to be a movie star when what he really wanted to be was a dictator. I'm not kidding. He wanted to rule China or Taiwan or somewhere!
Lee Marvin, 1924–1987, on Bruce Lee

She's certifiable!
Jack Nicholson, 1937–, on Faye Dunaway

When I met him, I wondered how he could possibly be qualified to direct this movie.
John Carradine, 1906–1988, on Woody Allen directing *Everything You Always Wanted To Know About Sex (But Were Afraid To Ask)*

Diana Ross doesn't want to do The Bodyguard, *because she wants to be white.*
Ryan O'Neal, 1941–, on Diana Ross

There were little boys around the house all the time... As far as his sexuality, he has never had a girlfriend, ever!
LaToya Jackson, 1954–, on Michael Jackson

Barbara Cartland's eyes were twin miracles of mascara and looked like two small crows that had crashed into a chalk cliff.
Clive James, 1939–, on Barbara Cartland and her make-up

Richard Gere and Cindy Crawford – he's elastic and she's plastic.
Sandra Bernhard, 1955–, on a match made in heaven

I was just really young. I don't know what his excuse is, but that's mine.
Winona Ryder, 1971–, on Johnny Depp

Will I have to be married to have kids? Maybe I won't be – just to piss off Dan Quayle.
Geena Davis, 1957–, on morality

I was particularly stunned by the casting of Cruise, who is no more my Vampire Lestat than Edward G. Robinson is Rhett Butler.
Anne Rice, 1941–, on the filming of *Interview With The Vampire* – she later

apologized and took out a full-page ad in the *New York Times* to say how perfect he was after all.

My mom told me that Robert Altman told her I have no personality. I have one – I must have one – but I don't quite know what it is.
Jennifer Jason Leigh, 1962–, suffering an identity crisis

For all Hollywood's fame and glamour, illusionary or otherwise, it does not have anything like a monopoly on the creative use of insulting invective. Perhaps the greatest wit the world has ever known was the Irish playwright and writer Oscar Fingal O'Flahertie Wills Wilde. The author of numerous plays, volumes of poetry, fairy tales, critical essays and one novel, he dazzled the social scenes in London and America. Flamboyant, incisive, funny and very, very quotable, Wilde made many friends, enemies and disciples. He was convicted of "homosexual offences" and imprisoned from 1895 to 1897, after which he moved from London to Paris, where he died a few years later. Despite the century which has passed since his fall from grace, he remains among the strongest literary influences on modern times. He wielded his dry sense of humour like a laser scalpel, putting aside tirades, rants, and clumsy obscenity to use instead reversed expectations and incisive observation against his targets. He held opinions on almost every area of life, from the philosophical...

There is much to be said in favour of modern journalism. By giving us the opinions of the uneducated, it keeps us in touch with the ignorance of the community.
Oscar Wilde, 1854–1900

Patriotism is the virtue of the vicious.
Oscar Wilde

Arguments are to be avoided; they are always vulgar, and often convincing.
Oscar Wilde

A cynic is a man who knows the price of everything and the value of nothing.
Oscar Wilde

Experience is the name everyone gives to their mistakes.
Oscar Wilde

A gentleman is one who never hurts anyone's feelings unintentionally.
Oscar Wilde

... to the societal. Even such deeply cherished institutions as friendship, family, marriage, romance and love were often in Wilde's sights.

Relations are simply a tedious pack of people who haven't got the remotest knowledge of how to live nor the smallest instinct about when to die.
Oscar Wilde

When one is in love, one begins by deceiving oneself, and one ends by deceiving others. This is what the world calls a romance.
Oscar Wilde, *A Woman of No Importance*

Men marry because they are tired, women because they are curious. Both are disappointed.
Ibid.

The amount of women in London who flirt with their own husbands is perfectly scandalous. It looks so bad. It is simply washing one's clean linen in public.
Oscar Wilde, on married couples

They flaunt their conjugal felicity in one's face, as if it were the most fascinating of sins.
Oscar Wilde, on married couples

Women love men for their defects; if men have enough of them, women will forgive them everything, even their gigantic intellects.
Oscar Wilde

I sometimes think that God, in creating man, somewhat overestimated his ability.
Oscar Wilde

Wilde cultivated a wide circle of genial enemies, sparring partners on whom he could focus his wit. The majority of them gave as good as they got, and there was quite a circle of these flamboyant, outspoken creatives all taking pot-shots at one another. We'll hear more from most of them in a little while.

Whistler has always spelt art with a capital I.
Oscar Wilde, on James Whistler

With our James, vulgarity begins at home – and should be allowed to stay there.
Oscar Wilde, on James Whistler

As for borrowing Mr Whistler's ideas about art, the only thoroughly original ideas I have ever heard him express have had reference to his own superiority as a painter over painters greater than himself.
Oscar Wilde, on James Whistler

Shaw hasn't become prominent enough to have any enemies, but none of his friends like him.
Oscar Wilde, on George Bernard Shaw

The gods have bestowed on Max the gift of perpetual old age.
Oscar Wilde, on Max Beerbohm

Another set of favourite targets for his scorn were America, Canada and England. They say that you shouldn't bite the hand that feeds you, but perhaps Wilde's charm was enough to let him get away with it.

Of course, America had often been discovered before Columbus, but it had always been hushed up.
Oscar Wilde, on America

It is absurd to say that there are neither ruins nor curiosities in America when they have their mothers and their manners.
Oscar Wilde, on America

In America, the president rules for four years and journalism governs for ever and ever.
Oscar Wilde, on America

America is one long expectoration.
Oscar Wilde, on America

When good Americans die they go to Paris; when bad Americans die, they go to America.
Oscar Wilde, on America, after Thomas Appleton

Niagara Falls is simply a vast, unnecessary amount of water going the wrong way and then falling over unnecessary rocks.
Oscar Wilde, on Niagara Falls, Canada

Every American bride is taken there, and the sight must be one of the earliest, if not the keenest disappointments of American married life.
Oscar Wilde, on Niagara Falls, Canada

Thinking is the most unhealthy thing in the world, and people die of it just as

they die of any other disease. Fortunately, in England at an rate, thought is not catching.
Oscar Wilde, on England

In England, it is enough for a man to try to produce any serious, beautiful work for him to lose all his rights as a citizen.
Oscar Wilde, on England

One of those characteristic British faces that, once seen, are never remembered.
Oscar Wilde

The English public takes no interest in a work of art until it is told that the work in question is immoral.
Oscar Wilde

Some of the funniest and cruellest of Wilde's jibes were aimed at people and places outside of his coterie.

Know him? I know him so well I haven't spoken to him for years.
Oscar Wilde

Please tell the cook of this restaurant with my compliments that these are the very worst sandwiches in the whole world and that, when I ask for a watercress sandwich, I do not mean a loaf with a field in the middle of it.
Oscar Wilde

I must decline your invitation owing to an engagement that I am just about to make.
Oscar Wilde

The play was a great success, but the audience was a disaster.
Oscar Wilde

He is old enough to know worse.
Oscar Wilde

It is perfectly scandalous the way people go about nowadays saying things against one, behind one's back, that are absolutely and entirely true.
Oscar Wilde

If this is the way Queen Victoria treats her prisoners, she doesn't deserve to have any.
Oscar Wilde, on life in prison

Like the man himself, most of Wilde's detractors spread their wit widely. Some of their ire focused on Oscar, but much more of it was generously distributed throughout all aspects of life.

Oscar Wilde's talent seems to me essentially rootless, something growing in a glass in a little water.
George Moore, 1852–1933, on Oscar Wilde

Wilde: I wish I had said that!
Whistler: You will, Oscar, you will.
James Whistler, 1834–1903, doubting the originality of Oscar Wilde's wit

What has Oscar in common with Art? Except that he dines at our tables and picks from our platters the plums for the pudding he peddles in the provinces. Oscar – the amiable, irresponsible, esurient Oscar – with no more sense of a picture than the fit of a coat has the courage of the opinions of others!
James Whistler, on Oscar Wilde

Mr Oscar Wilde is no poet, but a cleverish man who has an infinite contempt for his readers, and thinks he can take them in with a little mouthing verse.
The Spectator newspaper, 1881, on Oscar Wilde

James McNeill Whistler was one of Wilde's greatest friendly enemies. An American artist, he came to London in 1859 and took to the atmosphere immediately. His art was influenced by Japanese print techniques, and many members of the artistic establishment took great exception to his style. He sued a critic, John Ruskin, for libel; although the jury found in his favour, he was awarded offensively tiny damages of one farthing – the smallest coin available at the time. Another vocal member of this circle of literati was Maximilian Beerbohm, a caricaturist and author. An impatient perfectionist and critic, he fitted in well with the feel of the time.

Rossetti is not a painter. Rossetti is a ladies' maid.
James Whistler, on Dante Gabriel Rossetti

We are told that Mr Ruskin has devoted his long life to art, and as a result is Slade Professor at Oxford... A life passed among pictures does not make a painter – else the policeman in the National Gallery might assert himself... Let not Mr Ruskin flatter himself that more education makes the difference between himself and the policeman.
James Whistler, on John Ruskin

Why bring in Velasquez?
James Whistler, on being told that there were only two great painters, himself and Velasquez

I'm lonesome. They are all dying. I have hardly a warm personal enemy left.
James Whistler, on outliving his sparring partners

He would be all forgotten today if he had lived to be a florid old gentleman with iron-grey whiskers.
Max Beerbohm, 1872–1956, on Lord Byron

Of course, we all know that he was a wonderful all-round man, but the act of walking round him has always tired me.
Max Beerbohm, on William Morris

Reviewers seemed to fall into two classes: those who had little to say, and those that had nothing
Max Beerbohm

To mankind in general, Macbeth and Lady Macbeth stand out as the supreme type of all that a host and hostess should not be.
Max Beerbohm, on throwing dinner parties

If Wilde was the king of witty repartee, however, it was not Whistler or Beerbohm who claimed the title of Crown Prince, but George Bernard Shaw, another Irish playwright and author. A brilliant debater and dedicated socialist, his plays aimed both to entertain and to make the audience think about their social consciences. He was impatient and outspoken, and thought the English language hopelessly inconsistent. He campaigned, unsuccessfully, to get spelling standardized, and often wrote his plays using his own variant of English. He used to argue that "fish" could as well be spelt "ghoti", using "gh" from the word "rough", "o" from the word "women", and "ti" from the word "national". This eccentricity only added to his profile. As ready with a well-turned insult as Oscar Wilde, he tended to be slightly less pleasant.

He's a man of great common sense and good taste – meaning thereby a man without originality or moral courage.
George Bernard Shaw, 1856–1950

Do not do unto others as you would have them do unto you. Their tastes may not be the same.
George Bernard Shaw

I hate the poor, and I look forward eagerly to their extermination.
George Bernard Shaw, talking about the abolition of poverty, not murder

I am loath to interrupt the rapture of mourning in which the nation is now enjoying its favourite festive – a funeral – but in a country like ours the total suspension of common sense and sincere human feeling for a whole fortnight is an impossibility.
George Bernard Shaw, on the death of Queen Victoria

Music is the brandy of the damned.
George Bernard Shaw

Shaw: Would you sleep with a man for a million pounds?
Fellow guest, roguishly: That depends on how good-looking he was...
Shaw: How about for 10 shillings?
Fellow guest, horrified: What do you take me for?
Shaw: Madam, we have already settled that. Now we are negotiating over price.
George Bernard Shaw, terrorizing a lady whom he found himself next to over dinner...

A drama critic is a man who leaves no turn unstoned.
George Bernard Shaw, casting a stone at critics

Physically, there is nothing to distinguish human society from the farm-yard except that children are more troublesome and costly than chickens and women are not so completely enslaved as farm stock.
George Bernard Shaw, *Getting Married*

I have a technical objection to making sexual infatuation a tragic theme. Experience proves that it is only effective in the comic spirit.
George Bernard Shaw, *Three Plays For Puritans*

Like his fellow Irishman, George Bernard Shaw was highly critical of the English, and was prepared to take a swipe at America as well.

We don't bother much about dress and manners in England because as a nation we don't dress well and we've got no manners.
George Bernard Shaw, *You Never Can Tell*

The ordinary Britisher imagines that God is an Englishman.
George Bernard Shaw

Jews generally give great value. In my experience, the men who want something for nothing are invariably Christians.
George Bernard Shaw, *St Joan*

The whole strength of England lies in the fact that the enormous majority of the English people are snobs.
George Bernard Shaw, *Getting Married*

The 100% American is 99% idiot.
George Bernard Shaw

An Englishman does everything on principle; he fights you on patriotic principles; he robs you on business principles; he enslaves you on imperial principles.
George Bernard Shaw, *The Man of Destiny*

Our laws make law impossible, our liberties destroy all freedom, our property is organized robbery, our morality is an impudent hypocrisy, our wisdom is administered by inexperienced or malexperienced dupes, our power wielded by cowards and weaklings and our honour false in all its points. I am an enemy of the existing order for good reasons.
George Bernard Shaw, *Major Barbara*

When roused to irritation – never too unlikely a prospect – Shaw could be as cruel a critic of the person who sparked off his wrath as anyone else.

You have no nerve; you have no brain; you are the caricature of an eighteenth century male sentimentalist ... you are an owl, sickened by two days of my sunshine.
George Bernard Shaw, to Beatrice Stella Campbell

A more horrible offence against art than what you have put on the cover of the Essays has never been perpetrated, even in Newcastle.
George Bernard Shaw, to the printer of one of his works

It seems quite obvious that the real Brahms is nothing more than a sentimental voluptuary. He is the most wanton of composers. Only his wantonness is not vicious; it is that of a great baby, rather tiresomely addicted to dressing himself up as Handel or Beethoven and making a prolonged and intolerable noise.
George Bernard Shaw, on Johannes Brahms

A woman whose face looked as if it had been made of sugar and someone had licked it.
George Bernard Shaw, on Isadora Duncan

When one thinks of the donnish insolence and perpetual thick-skinned swagger of Chapman over his unique achievements in sublime balderdash ... it is hard to keep one's critical blood cool enough to discriminate in favour of any Elizabethan whatsoever.
George Bernard Shaw, on George Chapman

He is the true Elizabethan blank-verse beast, itching to frighten other people with the superstitious terrors and cruelties in which he himself does not believe, and wallowing in blood, violence, muscularity of expression and strenuous animal passion as only literary men do when they become thoroughly depraved by solitary

work, sedentary cowardice, and starvation of the sympathetic centres. It is not surprising to learn that Marlowe was stabbed in a tavern brawl: what would be utterly unbelievable would be his having succeeded in stabbing anyone else.
George Bernard Shaw, on Christopher Marlowe

Northcliffe: The trouble with you, Shaw, is that you look as if there were a famine in the land.
Shaw: The trouble with you, Northcliffe, is that you look as if you were the cause of it.
George Bernard Shaw, to Alfred Harmsworth, Lord Northcliffe

Perhaps because of his direct and uncompromising style, Shaw attracted a great deal of insults and criticisms. Some of these originated in literary circles, and related to his reviews or his books, while others were more personal.

When you were a little boy, someone ought to have said "Hush" just once.
Beatrice Stella Campbell, 1865–1940, to George Bernard Shaw

An Irish smut-dealer
Anthony Comstock, 1844–1915, on George Bernard Shaw

He writes like a Pakistani who has learned English when he was twelve years old in order to become an accountant.
John Osborne, 1929–1995, on George Bernard Shaw

An idiot child screaming in a hospital.
H.G. Wells, 1866–1946, on George Bernard Shaw

Shaw, most poisonous of all the poisonous haters of England; despiser, distorter and denier of the plain truths whereby men live; topsy-turvy perverter of all human relationships; a menace to ordered social life; irresponsible braggart,

blaring self-trumpeter; idol of opaque intellects and thwarted females; calculus of contrariwise; flipperty gibbet Pope of chaos; portent and epitome of this generation's moral and spiritual disorder.
Henry Jones, 1851–1929, on George Bernard Shaw

A freakish homunculus germinated outside lawful procreation.
Henry Jones, on George Bernard Shaw

The first man to have cut a swathe through the theatre and left it strewn with virgins.
Frank Harris, 1865–1931, on George Bernard Shaw

Intellectually he is beneath contempt. Artistically he appeals only to pseudo-philosophers. Are we not all a little tired of the blatant self-puffery?
Alfred Noyes, 1880–1958, on George Bernard Shaw

The way Shaw believes in himself is very refreshing, in these atheistic days when so many people believe in no God at all.
Israel Zangwill, 1864–1926, on George Bernard Shaw

A generation later than Shaw and Wilde, Noël Coward was a worthy inheritor of the mantle of the cultured detractor. Playwright, composer, director, actor and critic, he was genteel, mannered, bitterly sarcastic and often very funny. The archetypal sophisticated theatre man, he wrote and starred in plays, musicals and films on both sides of the Atlantic. After the Second World War, he started performing in nightclubs and revues, turning his particularly acidic brand of satire against the Establishment in songs of his own devising.

Miss Russell is a very metallic personality. She wants the impossible – nothing is good enough for her. I've decided not to work with her. Life is too short, and she's too long in the tooth and ego!
Noël Coward, 1899–1973, on Rosalind Russell

Keir Dullea, gone tomorrow.
Noël Coward, on Keir Dullea

An actor who has his head in the clouds and his feet in the box office.
Noël Coward, on Alfred Lunt

To be a moral thief, and unblushing liar, a supreme dictator, and a cruel, self-satisfied monster, and attain, in the minds of millions, the status of a deity is not only remarkable, but a dismal reflection on the human race. She had much in common with Hitler, only no moustache.
Noël Coward, on Mary Baker Eddy, founder of the Church of Christ Scientist

He is every other inch a gentleman.
Noël Coward, on an anonymous novelist

He's a little man, that's his trouble. Never trust a man with short legs – their brains are too near their bottoms.
Noël Coward, on height

It seems such a shame when the English claim the Earth, that they give rise to such hilarity and mirth.
Noël Coward, *Mad Dogs and Englishmen*

Two things in the play should have been cut – the second act and that youngster's throat.
Noël Coward

Blown his brains out, you say? He must have been an incredibly good shot.
Noël Coward

If Godfrey Winn offered you a cigarette it would be a bloody miracle.
Noël Coward, on Godfrey Winn

I should love to perform "There Are Fairies at the Bottom of our Garden", but I don't dare. It might come out "There Are Fairies in the Garden of my Bottom."
Noël Coward, on Bea Lillie's signature song

Mark Twain – born Samuel Langhorne Clemens – was one of America's greatest writers. *The Adventures of Huckleberry Finn* is widely regarded as his finest work; like his earlier novel *The Adventures of Tom Sawyer*, it is written in dialect and is a masterpiece of characterization and vernacular. He was also a cunning satirist and made extensive use of his sly humour throughout his writing. Given to bouts of pessimism, there were times when he was thoroughly negative about life in general.

Whoever has lived long enough to find out what life is knows how deep a debt of gratitude we owe Adam, the first great benefactor of our race. He brought death into the world.
Mark Twain, 1835–1910

Why is it we rejoice at a birth and grieve at a funeral? It is because we are not the person involved.
Mark Twain

All say how hard it is to die – a strange complaint from the mouths of people who have had to live.
Mark Twain

He was frequently uncomplimentary about individuals too, though. Always ready with a cutting put-down, Twain was a stern critic, and definitely not someone that you would have wanted to underwhelm.

Wagner's music is better than it sounds.
Mark Twain, on Richard Wagner

It is by the goodness of God that in our country we have those three unspeakably precious things: freedom of speech, freedom of conscience, and the prudence never to practice either of them.
Mark Twain

He wrote a doctor's hand – the hand which from the beginning of time has been so disastrous to the pharmacist and so profitable to the undertaker.
Mark Twain, on doctors

The critic's symbol should be the tumble-bug: he deposits his egg in somebody else's dung, otherwise he could not hatch it.
Mark Twain, on critics

A Frenchman's got a little standby for a dull time ... he can turn in and see if he can find out who his father was.
Mark Twain, on the French

Give an Irishman lager for a month and he's a dead man.
Mark Twain, on the Irish

Dorothy Parker was another brilliant American writer. A leading member of the literary circle called the Algonquin Round Table, she was an aphorist, critic and screenwriter. She had a wry, sharply cynical outlook on life, which she turned on leading public figures as often as on other targets.

To me, Edith looks like something that would eat its own young.
Dorothy Parker, 1893–1967, on Dame Edith Evans

She has only two expressions – joy and indigestion.
Dorothy Parker, on Marion Davies

How can they tell?
Dorothy Parker, on hearing that Calvin Coolidge was dead

Katharine Hepburn ran the whole gamut of emotions from A to B.
Dorothy Parker, on Katharine Hepburn

Two profiles pasted together.
Dorothy Parker, on Basil Rathbone

Where does she find them?
Dorothy Parker, on Clare Boothe Luce's social inferiors

Luce: Age before beauty!
Parker: Pearls before swine.
Dorothy Parker, graciously accepting Clare Boothe Luce's generous offer to let her through a doorway first

That woman speaks eighteen languages, and can't say "No" in any of them.
Dorothy Parker

As a literary critic, Parker was characteristically frank about her views, no matter how derogatory.

The affair between Margot Asquith and Margot Asquith will live as one of the prettiest love stories in all literature.
Dorothy Parker, on Margot Asquith's four-volume autobiography

And it is that word "hummy", my darlings, that marks the first place in The House at Pooh Corner *at which Tonstant Weader Fwowed Up.*
Dorothy Parker lampooning A.A. Milne in her "Constant Reader" column for the *New Yorker* newspaper

This is not a novel to be tossed aside lightly. It should be thrown with great force.
Ibid.

His ignorance was an Empire State Building of ignorance. You had to admire it for its size.
Dorothy Parker, on Harold Ross – founding editor of the *New Yorker* newspaper

Some of Parker's funniest and most bitter comments lie within her verses and other writings. No one before or since has captured quite the same spirit of resentful resignation about life.

Ducking for apples – change one letter and it's the story of my life.
Dorothy Parker being candidly modest

Guns aren't lawful,
Nooses give.
Gas smells awful.
Might as well live.
Dorothy Parker, on suicide

By the time you swear you're his,
Shivering and sighing,
And he vows his passion is
Infinite, undying,
Lady, make a note of this:
One of you is lying.
Dorothy Parker, *Unfortunate Coincidence*

You can lead a horticulture, but you cannot make her think.
Dorothy Parker, challenged to produce a sentence including the word "horticulture"

Every love's the love before, in a duller dress.
Dorothy Parker, *Summary*

A combination of Little Nell and Lady Macbeth.
Alexander Woolcott, 1887–1943, on Dorothy Parker

One of the great Romantic poets, William Wordsworth is relatively unusual in having attracted huge swathes of criticism without leaving any of his own invective behind. A great number of people have put a lot of effort into being nasty about him. He had an illegitimate daughter with a French woman, Anne-Marie Vallon, during his youth, before returning to England. He lived with his sister for the majority of his adult life, although he married in his early 30s. His detractors have taken an unflattering view of most of the different aspects of his life.

Wordsworth was a tea-time bore, the great Frost of literature, the verbose, the humourless, the platitudinary reporter of Nature in her dullest moods.
Dylan Thomas, 1914–1953, on William Wordsworth

Wordsworth has left a bad impression wherever he visited in town by his egotism, vanity and bigotry.
John Keats, 1795–1821, on William Wordsworth

In his youth, Wordsworth sympathized with the French Revolution, went to France, wrote good poetry, and had a natural daughter. At this period, he was a "bad" man. Then he became "good", abandoned his daughter, adopted correct principles, and wrote bad poetry.
Bertrand Russell, 1872–1970, on William Wordsworth

He both by precept and example shows
That prose is verse, and verse is merely prose.
Lord Byron, 1788–1824, on William Wordsworth

Let simple Wordsworth chime his childish verse.
Lord Byron, on William Wordsworth

A stupid man, with a decided gift for portraying nature in vignettes, never yet ruined anyone's morals, unless, perhaps, he has driven some susceptible persons to crime in a very fury of boredom.
Ezra Pound, 1885–1972, on William Wordsworth

Is Wordsworth a bell with a wooden tongue?
Ralph Waldo Emerson, 1803–1882, on William Wordsworth

For prolixity, thinness, endless dilution, it excels all the other speech I had heard from mortals. The languid way in which he gives you a handful of numb, unresponsive fingers is very significant.
Thomas Carlyle, 1795–1881, on William Wordsworth

The inner, the conversational and private has many coarse intractable dangling threads, fit only for the flockbed equipage of grooms.
Walter Landor, 1775–1864, on William Wordsworth

Dank, limber verses, stuffed with lakeside sedges,
And propped with rotten stakes from rotten hedges.
Walter Landor, on William Wordsworth

An old, half-witted sheep which bleats articulate monotony.
James Kenneth Stephen, 1859–1892, on William Wordsworth

Another writer who has been roundly savaged is James Joyce. A brilliant Irish author, he displayed real literary genius in his work. *Ulysses* made use of revolutionary stream-of-consciousness techniques, experimenting with language itself, as it charted the course of one single Dublin day through the eyes of several different characters. It combined narrative with unspoken thought and unconscious reaction on the part of the characters. It was banned in the UK and USA on release because of its "obscenity", guaranteeing it a high profile. *Finnegan's Wake*, published 17 years later, was even more experimental – so much so that even today scholars are arguing about exactly what it was Joyce meant. At the time, though, there were plenty of commentators who felt they knew *exactly* what he meant, and were not afraid of saying so.

It is written by a man with a diseased mind and soul so black that he would obscure even the darkness of hell.
Senator Reed Smoot, 1862–1941, on James Joyce

I have difficulty in describing the character of Mr Joyce's morality. He is a literary charlatan of the extremist order. His principal book, Ulysses, *is an anarchical production, infamous in taste, in style, in everything. He is a sort of Marquis de Sade, but does not write as well.*
Edmund Gosse, 1849–1928, on James Joyce

There are no English critics of any weight or judgement who consider Mr Joyce an author of any importance.
Edmund Gosse, on James Joyce

Never have I read such tosh. As for the first two chapters we will let them pass, but the 3rd, 4th, 5th, 6th – merely the scratchings of pimples on the body of the bootboy at Claridges.
Virginia Woolf, 1882–1941, on James Joyce

The work of a queasy undergraduate.
Virginia Woolf, on James Joyce

Probably Joyce thinks that because he prints all the dirty little words, he is a great hero.
George Moore, 1852–1933, on James Joyce

My God, what a clumsy olla putrida *James Joyce is! Nothing but old fags and cabbage-stumps of quotations from the Bible and the rest, stewed in the juice of deliberate, journalistic dirty-mindedness.*
D.H. Lawrence, 1885–1930, on James Joyce

The last part of it is the dirtiest, most indecent, most obscene thing ever written ... it is filthy.
D.H. Lawrence, on James Joyce

There is a certain irony to D.H. Lawrence's revulsion with James Joyce, because he himself was frequently slated as filthy, obscene and perverted. His most famous novel was *Lady Chatterley's Lover*, which was banned in the UK as obscene and pornographic from 1928 to 1960. He had run away with and later married the wife of his university professor, and he believed strongly that the sexual impulse was a true, creative expression of human nature. The deregulation of *Lady Chatterley's Lover* contributed greatly to the era of sexual liberation through the 1960s and 70s, and has therefore had a profound effect on today's society. Critics levelled the same sort of charges at Lawrence that he himself had aimed at Joyce.

Mr Lawrence has a diseased mind. He is obsessed by sex and we have no doubt that he will be ostracized by all except the most degenerate coteries of the world.
John Bull magazine, 1928, on D.H. Lawrence

Is anything in life or literature past or present in earth, heaven or hell, anything more devastatingly tedious than D.H.L'.s interest in the human genitalia?
G.W. Lyttelton, 1878–1963, on D.H. Lawrence

Lawrence is in a long line of people, beginning with Heraclitus and ending with Hitler, whose ruling motive is hatred derived from megalomania.
Bertrand Russell, 1872–1970, on D.H. Lawrence

Lawrence represented the last phase of the Romantic movement: random, irresponsible egotism, power for power's sake, the blood cult of Rosenberg.
V.S. Pritchett, 1900 –, on D.H. Lawrence

Lawrence was certainly an evil-tempered terror when his ire was roused. His attacks were thunderous and pulled no punches; when it came to being offensive, he went straight for the throat, bared fangs dripping acidic saliva.

Curse the blasted, jelly-boned swines, the slimy, the belly-wriggling invertebrates, the miserable sodding rotters, the flaming sods, the snivelling, dribbling, dithering, palsied, pulseless lot that make up England today. They've got white of egg in their veins, and their spunk is so watery it's a marvel they can breed. They can produce nothing but frogspawn – the gibberers. God, how I hate them! Why, why, why was I born an Englishman?
D.H. Lawrence, 1885–1930 on England, after having a manuscript rejected

I loathe you. You revolt me, stewing in your consumption. The Italians were quite right to have nothing to do with you.
D.H. Lawrence, to Katherine Mansfield

Spit on her for me when you see her, she's a liar out and out. As for him, I reserve my language. Vermin, the pair of them.
D.H. Lawrence, on Katherine Mansfield and her lover, J. Middleton Murray

The enemy of all mankind, you are, full of the lust of enmity. It is not hatred of falsehood which inspires you. It is the hatred of people, of flesh and blood. It is perverted, mental bloodlust. Why don't you own up to it?
D.H. Lawrence, to Bertrand Russell

Kick all America in the guts: they need it. Spit on every neurotic, and wipe your feet on his face if he tries to drag you down to him. All that "arty" and "literary" crew, I know them, they are smoking, steaming shits.
D.H. Lawrence, on the American literary scene

This awful Whitman, this post-mortem poet. This poet with the private soul leaking out of him all the time. All his privacy leaking out in a sort of dribble, oozing into the universe.
D.H. Lawrence, on Walt Whitman

Too much a gas-bag.
D.H. Lawrence, mildly criticizing George Bernard Shaw

Bennett – sort of a pig in clover.
D.H. Lawrence, on Arnold Bennett

Appropriately, the final say in this section belongs to Virginia Woolf. An important novelist and critic with a strong feminist streak, which she often explored in her books, she was a major figure in the British literary scene during the first half of the twentieth century. Often prone to fits of depression – she eventually took her own life – she was, none the less, a very dangerous opponent in any verbal war, and she always was keen to have the last word.

Pale, marmoreal Eliot was there last week, like a chapped office boy on a high stool, with a cold in his head.
Virginia Woolf, 1882–1941, on T.S. Eliot

He is limp and damp and milder than the breath of a cow.
Virginia Woolf, on E.M. Forster

No-one has written worse English than Mr Hardy in some of his novels – stilted, cumbrous, ugly and inexpressive.
Virginia Woolf, on Thomas Hardy

All raw, uncooked, protesting.
Virginia Woolf, on Aldous Huxley

We could both wish that our first impression of KM was not that she stinks like a – well, civet cat that had taken to street walking. In truth, I'm a little shocked by her commonness at first sight; lines so hard and cheap.
Virginia Woolf, on Katherine Mansfield

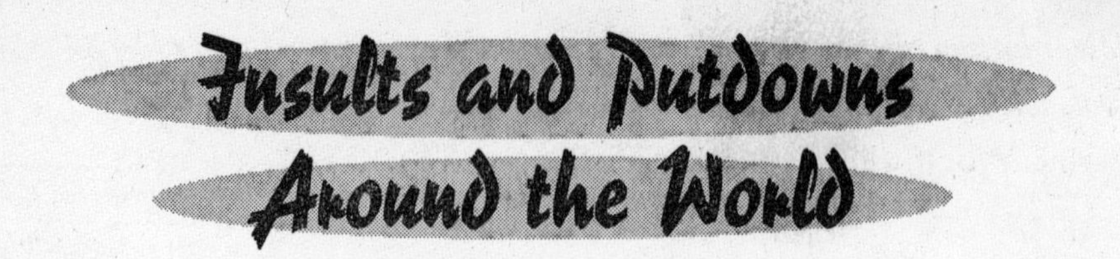

You'll never find a more wretched hive of scum and villainy – we must be cautious.
Brendon Douglas, 1972–, on Basingstoke, England, citing George Lucas, 1944–, *Star Wars*

Nationalism is a funny thing. Borders and boundaries change all the time, new countries appear out of old ones, just to be swallowed up again, smaller states clump together into larger ones and then split back up again in new configurations. Wars are particularly notorious for changing the shape of the political map. If you look back a thousand years, almost none of the nations we currently know would have existed; even a hundred years ago, things were greatly different in a number of places. Despite this, most people feel a strong loyalty and reverence for their country. Having a nationality is about being part of something bigger than the individual, of having common bonds. Looking at this next section of quotes, though, you'll see that one of the favourite ways of defining a group is by insulting everything outside of it – particularly the neighbours.

For most nations, the country next door is an object of historical scorn. Chances are, border wars have been fought in the past, and the real advantage of using nearby countries as a target is that they're close enough to identify the most effective bits to criticize. The rivalry between the English and the French is legendary, like that between the Germans and the Poles, the Spanish and the Portuguese, the Greeks and the Turks, the ... but the list could go on and on and on. For every nation on earth, someone somewhere has been extremely rude about it. Stereotypes are slandered, customs are ridiculed, and the people made fun of. Fortunately, the great majority of people treat national rivalry with a healthy lack of seriousness. Below, some of the most amusing and offensive slurs against national identity from around the globe have been collected. Enjoy them, but don't be surprised if you find that you're laughing at your own back yard.

Heaven has English police, French cooking, German engineering, Italian lovers, Dutch laws and Swiss organization. Hell, on the other hand, has English cooking, German police, Italian laws, French engineering, Dutch organization, and Swiss lovers.
Anonymous

Of all the nations, Great Britain – both collectively and in its constituent parts – has been the unhappy recipient of more insults than any other. There seems to be something about the UK that arouses fury in otherwise perfectly sane members of a wide variety of societies all over the globe. Of course, any country that expands its influence to establish a restrictive empire worldwide is going to make a lot of enemies, particularly when it comes to the perceived maltreatment of conquered countries. There were other developments, too, that perhaps were asking for trouble – as the cradle of the Industrial Revolution, for example, Great Britain is largely responsible for the current state of society. It was Britons and their descendants who shaped the USA, Canada, Australia, and New Zealand. The weather's absolutely dreadful, as well. But surely that's not enough to warrant all this invective ... is it?

Paralytic sycophants.
Effete betrayers of humanity.
Carrion-eating servile imitators.
Arch-cowards and collaborators.
Gang of women-murderers.
Degenerate rabble.
Parasitic traditionalists.

Playboy soldiers.
Conceited dandies.
Official communist East German terms sanctioned for use in describing Britain, *c.* 1951

A pirate spreading misery and ruin over the face of the Earth.
Thomas Jefferson, 1743–1826, on Britain

In Germany, democracy died by the headsman's axe. In Britain, it can be killed by pernicious anaemia.
Aneurin Bevan, 1897–1960, on the boredom of English politics

A nation of ants, morose, frigid, and still preserving the same dread of happiness and joy as in the days of John Knox.
Paul Blouet, 1848–1903, on Britain

We know of no spectacle so ridiculous as the British public in one of its periodic fits of morality.
Thomas Macaulay, 1800–1859

It is true that they take pleasure in seeing gladiators fight, in seeing bulls torn to pieces by dogs, seeing cocks fight, and that in the carnivals they use batons against the cocks, but it is not out of cruelty so much as coarseness.
G. le Sage, 1668–1747, on Britain

You must look out in Britain that you are not cheated by the charioteers.
Cicero, 106–43BC

The two sides of industry have traditionally always regarded each other in Britain with the greatest possible loathing, mistrust and contempt. They are both absolutely right.
Auberon Waugh, 1939–, on British labour relations

Sheep with a nasty side.
Cyril Connolly, 1903–1974, on the British

The majority of the insults slung at Britain have been specifically aimed at the English. The Scots, Welsh and Irish are responsible for much of it, grudges for old insults and injuries lovingly nursed down through the centuries. The French, too, have always been quick to slander *Les Rosbifs.* But they're not the only ones – not by a long way. The English are accused of a vast range of sins. To some commentators, the English are cowardly and unpleasant:

Poltroons, cowards, skulkers and dastards.
Eugene Deschamps, 1346–1406, on England

England, the heart of a rabbit in the body of a lion, the jaws of a serpent in an abode of popinjays.
Eugene Deschamps, on England

The perfidious, haughty, savage, disdainful, stupid, slothful, inhospitable, inhuman English.
Julius Scaliger, 1540–1609, on England

Unmitigated noodles.
Kaiser Wilhelm II, 1859–1941, on England

The English are, I think, the most obtuse and barbarous people in the world.
Stendhal, 1783–1842

What a pity it is that we have no amusements in England but vice and religion.
Sydney Smith, 1771–1845

It must be acknowledged that the English are the most disagreeable of all the nations of Europe, more surly and morose, with less disposition to please, to exert themselves for the good of society, to make small sacrifices, and to put themselves out of their way.
Sydney Smith

The English talk loudly and seem to care little for other people. This is their characteristic, and a very brutal and barbarous distinction it is.
Sydney Smith

England has become a squalid, uncomfortable, ugly place – an intolerant, racist, homophobic, narrow-minded, authoritarian, rat-hole run by vicious, suburban-minded, materialistic philistines.
Hanif Kureishi, 1954–

For others, the English are totally unreliable, far too fixated with money, and not to be trusted under any circumstances.

Like an English oath.
Dutch saying, meaning "it is worthless"

We're no longer a nation of shopkeepers; we're a nation of cowboys.
Kirsty MacColl, 1957–, on the unreliability of English businesses

Among three Italians will be found two clergymen; among three Spaniards two braggarts; among three Germans two soldiers; among three Frenchmen two chefs; and among three Englishmen two whoremongers.
German saying

Do you speak English?
Spanish way of asking "do you have any money?"

In all the four corners of the earth, one of these three names is given to him who steals from his neighbour – brigand, robber or Englishman.
Les Triades del Anglais, 1572, on England

A demon took a monkey to wife – the result, by the grace of God, was the English.
Indian saying

The German originates it, the Frenchman imitates it, and the Englishman exploits it.
German saying

The English are, in my opinion, perfidious and cunning, plotting the destruction of the lives of foreigners, so that even if they humbly bend the knee, they cannot be trusted.
Leo de Rozmital, 1468–1510

I know why the sun never sets on the British Empire: God wouldn't trust an Englishman in the dark.
Duncan Spaeth, 1868–1954

The English have no exalted sentiment. They can all be bought.
Napoleon Bonaparte, 1769–1821

The weather is appalling; many detractors are in no doubt that it's the cause of most of the English sins.

The way to endure summer in England is to have it framed and glazed in a comfortable room.
Horace Walpole, 1717–1797

It is cowardly to commit suicide. The English often kill themselves – it is a malady caused by the humid climate.
Napoleon Bonaparte

From England comes neither fair wind nor good war.
French saying

Given the weather, it should come as no surprise to find that several peoples consider the English almost painfully lazy. After all, they're probably all in bed trying to keep out of the rain. When they are up and about though, they are supposed to be either eating, drinking, or sitting around indulging in other bad habits.

An Englishman will burn in his bed to catch a flea.
Turkish saying

They are naturally lazy, and spend half their time in taking tobacco.
Samuel de Sorbière, 1615–1670, on the English

The Englishman is a drunkard.
Spanish saying

It is related of an Englishman that he hung himself to avoid the daily task of dressing and undressing.
Johann Wolfgang von Goethe, 1749–1832

Gluttony is the sin of England
English saying

London, black as crows and as noisy as ducks, prudish with all the vices in evidence, everlastingly drunk, in spite of ridiculous laws about drunkenness, immense, though it is really basically only a collection of scandal-mongering

boroughs vying with each other, ugly and dull, without any monuments except interminable docks.
Paul Verlaine, 1844–1896

The food in England, according to much of the rest of the world, is as nasty as the weather...

Go back, you dissolute English. Drink your beer and eat your pickled beef.
La Repentance des Anglais et des Espagnols, c. 1522

The average cooking in the average hotel for the average Englishman explains to a large extent the English bleakness and taciturnity. Nobody can beam and warble while chewing pressed beef smeared with diabolical mustard. Nobody can exult aloud while ungluing from his teeth a quivering tapioca pudding.
Karel Capek, 1890–1938

The English, who eat their meat red and bloody, show the savagery that goes with such food.
J. De la Mettrie, 1709–1751

Belching at table, and in all companies whatsoever, is a thing which the English no more scruple than they do coughing and sneezing.
H. Misson de Valbourg, 1656–1723

There are in England sixty different religious sects and only one sauce.
Caracciolo, 1572–1641

The depressing thing about an Englishman's traditional love of animals is the dishonesty thereof – get a barbed hook into the upper lip of a salmon, drag him endlessly around the water until he loses his strength, pull him to the bank, hit him on the head with a stone, and you may well become

fisherman of the year. Shoot the salmon and you'll never be asked again.
Clement Freud, 1924–

... and the language is apparently horrid.

The devil take these people and their language! They take a dozen monosyllabic words in their jaws, chew them, crunch them and spit them out again, and call that speaking. Fortunately they are by nature fairly silent, and although they gaze at us open-mouthed, they spare us long conversations.
Heinrich Heine, 1797–1856

These people have no ear, either for rhythm or music, and their unnatural passion for pianoforte playing and singing is thus all the more repulsive. There is nothing on earth more terrible than English music, except English painting.
Heinrich Heine

Silence – a conversation with an Englishman.
Heinrich Heine

To learn English you must begin by thrusting the jaw forward, almost clenching the teeth, and practically immobilizing the lips. In this way the English produce the series of unpleasant little mews of which their language consists.
Jose Ortega y Gasset, 1883–1955

All Englishmen talk as if they've got a bushel of plums stuck in their throats, and then after swallowing them get constipated from the pits.
W.C. Fields, 1879–1946

As if that wasn't bad enough, there's also the fact – according to the world at large – that the English aren't actually any good at anything much. A rather, dull, mediocre bunch, if other countries are to be believed.

From every Englishman emanates a kind of gas, the deadly choke-damp of boredom.
Heinrich Heine

The English instinctively admire any man who has no talent and is modest about it.
James Agate, 1877–1947

England will fight to the last American.
American saying

Freedom of speech in England is little else than the right to write or say anything which a jury of twelve shopkeepers think it expedient should be said or written.
A. Dicey, 1835–1922

Only Englishmen and dogs walk in the sun.
Italian saying

In our English popular religion the common conception of a future state of bliss is that of a kind of perfected middle-class home, with labour ended, the table spread, goodness all around, the lost ones restored – hymnody incessant.
Matthew Arnold, 1822–1888, on the English view of Heaven

Thirty millions, mostly fools.
Thomas Carlyle, 1795–1881, on the population of England

The English think that incompetence is the same thing as sincerity.
Quentin Crisp, 1908–

The moment the name of Ireland is mentioned, the English seem to bid adieu to common feeling, common prudence, and common sense, and to act with the barbarity of tyrants and the fatuity of idiots.
Sydney Smith

It is only necessary to raise a bugbear before the English imagination in order to govern it at will. Whatever they hate or fear, they implicitly believe in.
William Hazlitt, 1778–1830

Those little social skills and cultural niceties that other countries take for granted seem often to be thought of as strangely lacking from the English make-up, too.

The English think soap is civilization.
Heinrich von Treitschke, 1833–1896

English windows open only half-way, either the top half or the bottom half. One may even have the pleasure of opening them a little at the top and a little at the bottom, but not at all in the middle. The sun cannot enter openly, nor the air. The window keeps its selfish and perfidious character. I hate the English windows.
Sarah Bernhardt, 1844–1896

Englishwomen's shoes look as if they had been made by someone who had often heard shoes described, but had never seen any.
Margaret Halsey, 1878–1947

The English are not a sculptural nation.
N. Pevsner, 1902–1983

Continental people have a sex life. The English have hot-water bottles.
George Mikes, 1912–, on the difference between England and the rest of Europe

In the eyes of the Englishman, the Frenchman is a dog, the Spaniard a fool, the German a drunkard, the Italian a bandit, only the Englishman is the pinnacle of perfection, and nature's masterpiece.
A. Riem, 1762–1828

Long beards heartless, painted hoods witless, gay coats graceless, make England thriftless.
Scottish saying

A broad definition of crime in England is that it is any lower-class activity that is displeasing to the upper class.
David Frost, 1939–, and Anthony Jay, 1930–, *To England With Love*

Although it is currently rather fashionable on the world scene, Scotland has also had a more-than-generous share of detractors. The country itself has often been characterized as ugly, forbidding and inhospitable, and the weather is even worse than it is in England. One of Scotland's harshest critics has been Dr Samuel Johnson, who not only loathed the place with an unholy passion, but said so constantly, too.

The great thing about Glasgow now is that if there's a nuclear attack, it'll look exactly the same afterwards.
Billy Connolly, 1942–, on Glasgow, Scotland

It is a very vile country.
Samuel Johnson, 1709–1784, on Scotland

God made it, but we must remember that He made it for Scotchmen; and comparisons are odious, but God made Hell.
Samuel Johnson, on Scotland

That garret of the earth, the knuckle-end of England, that land of Calvin, oat-cakes and sulphur.
Sydney Smith, on Scotland

Oats: a grain which, in England, is generally given to horse, but in Scotland supports the people.
Samuel Johnson

It requires a surgical operation to get a joke well into a Scotch understanding.
Sydney Smith

Of course, the Scots are known worldwide for being cautious with their money. To be more accurate, they have the reputation for being mean, uncharitable, tight-fisted, ungenerous, and at least as unlikely to buy a round of drinks as any other nationality.

The Scotsman is one who keeps the Sabbath and everything else he can lay his hands on.
American saying

I have been trying all my life to like Scotchmen, and am obligated to desist from the experiment in despair.
Charles Lamb, 1775–1834

Jews, Scotsmen and counterfeits will be encountered throughout the world.
German saying

As hard-hearted as a Scot of Scotland.
English saying

Scotsmen take all they can get – and a little more, if they can.
Scottish saying

There are few more impressive sights than a Scotsman on the make.
James Barrie, 1860–1937

It is possible that all Scots are illegitimate, Scotsmen being so mean and Scotswomen being so generous.
English saying

Give a Scotsman an inch and he'll take a mile.
Scottish saying

Of all the component sections of the UK, however, the most universally slated are the Welsh. The English don't much like them, but that's no real surprise – the English often don't much like anyone. The Scots and the Irish, though, who are normally fairly united in disliking England and liking each other, also look down on Wales. Even the Welsh seem to dislike the Welsh...

The earth contains no race of human beings so totally vile and worthless as the Welsh. I have expended in labour, within three years, nearly eight thousand pounds amongst them, yet they treat me as their greatest enemy.
Walter Savage Landor, 1775–1864

Taffy was a Welshman, Taffy was a thief,
Taffy came into my house and stole a side of beef.
English nursery rhyme

A Welshman prays on his knees on a Sunday and preys on his friends the rest of the week.
English saying

They are treacherous to each other as well as to foreigners, covet freedom, neglect peace, are warlike and skilful in arms, and are eager for revenge.
Walter Map, 1140–1209

The older the Welshman, the more a madman.
English saying

Each section of the British Isles has its own way of laughing, except Wales, which doesn't.
Stephen Leacock, 1869–1944

The ordinary women of Wales are generally short and squat, ill-favoured and nasty.
David Mallet, 1705–1765

The Welsh are so damn Welsh that it looks like affectation.
Sir Alexander Raleigh, 1861–1922

The land of my fathers – and my fathers can have it.
Dylan Thomas, 1914–1953, on Wales

There are still parts of Wales where the only concession to gaiety is a striped shroud.
Gwyn Thomas, 1913–1981

There are characteristics associated with the Irish that are known worldwide. Lucky, charming, and witty, they must have been blessed by God, it would seem. Not everyone agrees, though, and if they're known for their supposed gift of the gab, they're also known for stupidity, excessive drinking, quick tempers and treachery!

It's totally Irish.
English saying, meaning something is stupid or illogical

An Irish homosexual is one who prefers women to drink.
Sean O'Faolain, 1956–

The Irish are a fair-minded people – they never speak well of one another.
Samuel Johnson

Put an Irishman on the spit, and you can always get another Irishman to turn him.
George Bernard Shaw, 1856–1950

The Irish, the Irish, they don't amount to much,
But they're a darn sight better than the dirty, dirty Deutch.
American rhyme

For the Irish, there are no stars in the sky.
English saying

A servile race in folly nursed.
Jonathan Swift, 1667–1745, on the Irish

Like an Irishman's obligation – all on the one side, and always yours.
English saying

If one could only teach the English how to talk and the Irish how to listen, society would be quite civilized.
Oscar Wilde, 1854–1900

As sluttish and slatternly as an Irish woman raised in France.
Irish saying

The problem with Ireland is that it's a country full of genius with absolutely no talent.
Hugh Leonard, 1925–

The United States seems to inspire at least as much hatred as Britain and Ireland, of course. Maybe it's the loud, over-familiar nature of American tourists, which always startles Europeans, that is the problem. Maybe it's the frighteningly tasteless Bermuda shorts those same tourists are wearing. Maybe it's their hamburger restaurants, or their lawyers, or their guns. Whatever the reason, the USA is a favourite punch-bag for the world. There are almost no depths of depravity that Americans won't – supposedly – sink to:

Violence is as American as cherry pie.
Stokely Carmichael, 1941–

Knavery seems to be so much the striking feature of its inhabitants that it may not in the end be an evil that they will become aliens to this country.
George III, 1738–1820, on America

They are a race of convicts and ought to be grateful for anything we allow them short of hanging.
Samuel Johnson, on America

Frustrate a Frenchman, and he will drink himself to death; an Irishman, and he will die of angry hypertension; a Dane, and he will shoot himself; an American, and he will get drunk, shoot you, then establish a million-dollar aid programme for your relatives. Then he will die of an ulcer.
S. Rudin, 1938–1994

America is the only nation in history which miraculously has gone directly from barbarism to degeneration without the usual interval of civilization.
Georges Clemenceau, 1841–1929

A city of 7,000,000 so decadent that when I leave it, I never dare look back lest I turn into a pillar of salt and the conductor throw me over

his left shoulder for good luck.
Frank Sullivan, 1903–1977, on New York

The American character always looks as if it just had a rather bad haircut.
Mary McCarthy, 1912–

The American people are clannish, insular and inward looking, apparently.

Every time Europe looks across the Atlantic to see the American eagle, it observes only the rear end of an ostrich.
H.G.Wells, 1886–1946

I am willing to love all mankind except an American.
Samuel Johnson, his hate-affair with the Scots plainly slipping his mind for the moment.

Their demeanour is invariably morose, sullen, clownish and repulsive. I should think there is not on the face of the earth a people so entirely destitute of humour, vivacity or the capacity of enjoyment.
Charles Dickens, 1812–1870, on Americans

I suppose there is less alms-giving in America than in any other Christian country on the face of the globe. It is not in the temper of the people either to give or to receive.
Frances Trollope, 1780–1863

The American has no language. He has dialect, slang, provincialism, accent and so forth.
Rudyard Kipling, 1865–1936

You are right in your impression that a number of persons are urging me to come to the United States. But why on earth do you call them my friends?
George Bernard Shaw, on being invited to America

All American writing gives me the impression that Americans don't care for girls at all. What the American male really wants is two things: he wants to be blown by a stranger while reading a newspaper, and he wants to be fucked by his buddy when he's drunk. Everything else is society.
W.H. Auden, 1907–1973

If you're going to America, bring your own food.
Fran Lebowitz, 1951–

In the four corners of the globe, who reads an American book? Or goes to an American play? Or looks at an American picture or statue? What does the world yet owe to America's physicians and surgeons? Who drinks out of American glasses? Or eats from American plates? Or wears American coats and gowns? Or sleeps in American blankets? Under which of the old tyrannical governments of Europe is every sixth man a slave, whom his fellow creatures may buy and sell and torture?
Sydney Smith

Greater yet, however, in terms of nation sin, is the American preoccupation with money. Dollars, greenbacks, filthy lucre, shemolah, dosh, whatever you call it, it seems to be an obsession – one the rest of the world disapproves of, or pretends to, at least.

I heard an Englishman, who had been long resident in America, declare that in following, in meeting, or in overtaking, in the street, on the road, or in the field, at the theatre, the coffee-house, or at home, he had never heard Americans conversing without the word "dollar" being pronounced between them.
Frances Trollope

There is a constant activity going on in one small portion of the brain; all the rest is stagnant. Their money-making faculty is alone cultivated. They are incapable of acquiring general knowledge on a broad or liberal scale. All is confined to trace, finance, law, and small, local provincial information. Art, science, literature, are nearly dead letters to them.
T. Grattan, 1792–1864, on Americans

Americans are people who laugh at African witch doctors and then spend 100 million dollars on fake reducing systems.
L.L. Levinson, 1932–

If there ever was an aviary overstocked with jays it is that Yaptown on the Hudson called New York.
O. Henry, 1862–1910, on New York

When the American people are not talking about money – maybe one minute in each day, apparently – they are instead spitting on the floor, being rude and ill-mannered, and serving up the most frightful food...

No one can be as calculatedly rude as the British, which amazes Americans, who do not understand studied insult and can only offer abuse as a substitute.
Paul Gallico, 1897–1976

The European continent swarms with your people. They are not all as polished as Chesterfield. I wish some of them spoke French a little better. I saw five of them at supper at Basle the other night with their knives down their throats. It was awful.
William Makepeace Thackeray, 1811–1863, on American eating habits

The total want of all the usual courtesies of the table, the voracious rapidity with which the viands were seized and devoured; the strange uncouth phrases and pronunciation; the loathsome spitting, from the contamination of which

it was absolutely impossible to protect our dresses; the frightful manner of feeding with their knives, till the whole blade seemed to enter into the mouth, and the still more frightful manner of cleaning the teeth afterwards with a pocket-knife, soon forced us to feel that ... the dinner-hour was to be anything rather than an hour of enjoyment.
Frances Trollope, on Americans at the dining table

You can never conceive what the hawking and spitting is the whole night through. Last night was the worst. Upon my honour and word, I was obliged, this morning, to lay my fur coat on the deck and wipe the half-dried flakes of spittle from it with my handkerchief. The only surprise seemed to be that I should consider it necessary to do so. When I turned in last night, I put it on a stool beside me, and there it lay, under a crossfire from five men – three opposite; one above; and one below. I made no complaints and showed no disgust.
Charles Dickens, on the American habit of spitting

I hardly know any annoyance so deeply repugnant to English feelings as the incessant, remorseless spitting of Americans.
Frances Trollope, on the American habit of spitting

Every broken down barber or disappointed dancing master, French, German or Italian, sets up as a cook with about as much knowledge of cookery as a cow has of cucumbers. In a word, the science of the table is at the earliest stage of infancy in the United States.
T. Grattan, on American cuisine

When you become used to never being alone, you may consider yourself Americanized.
André Maurois, 1885–1967

The citizens of the United States are also sadly lacking in their interpersonal skills, if the critics are to be believed.

The Americans ... probably make love worse than any other race.
Walt Whitman, 1819–1892

The American male doesn't mature until he has exhausted all other possibilities.
Wilfred Sheed, 1934–

American women hope to find in their husbands the perfection that English women only expect to find in their butlers.
Somerset Maugham, 1874–1965

I never saw an American man walk or stand well – they are nearly all hollow chested and round shouldered.
Frances Trollope

The ladies have strange ways of adding to their charms. They powder themselves immoderately, face, neck, and arms, with pulverized starch; the effect is indescribably disagreeable by daylight, and not very favourable at any time.
Frances Trollope

In fact, when you get down to it, the USA is just plain unsatisfactory.

Interviewer: If you find so much that is unworthy of reverence in the United States, why do you live here?
Mencken: Why do men go to zoos?
H.L. Mencken, 1880–1956, on America

The trouble with America is that there are far too many wide open spaces surrounded by teeth.
Charles Luckman, 1909–

Speaking of New York as a traveller, I have two faults to find with it. In the first place there is nothing to see; and in the second place there is no mode of getting about to see anything.
Anthony Trollope, 1815–1882

The method of heating many of the best houses is a terrible grievance to persons not accustomed to it, and a fatal misfortune to those who are. Casual visitors are nearly suffocated, and constant occupiers killed.
T. Grattan, on American central heating

The thing that impresses me most about America is the way parents obey their children.
The Duke of Windsor, 1894–1972

Canada finds herself in a strange position, and not just by being to the north of the USA. The bulk of the world's commentators seem to consider the country beneath notice, and then go on to talk and write at great length about exactly how irrelevant Canada actually is. This seems to be missing the point, somehow...

You know that these two nations are at war for a few acres of snow, and that they are spending more than all Canada is worth.
Voltaire, 1694–1778, on Canada

Canada is useful only to provide me with furs.
Madame de Pompadour, 1721–1764

I fear that I have not got much to say about Canada, not having seen much; what I got by going to Canada was a cold.
Henry David Thoreau, 1817–1862

A Canadian is someone who knows how to make love in a canoe.
Pierre Berton, 1862–1933, on Canada

This gloomy region, where the year is divided into one day and one night, lies entirely outside the stream of history.
W.W. Reade, 1814–1884, on Canada

Fellow citizens, this country is going to the dogs hand over hand.
T.C. Haliburton, 1795–1861, on Canada

Canada is America's attic.
Robertson Davies, 1871–1940

Canada is also reputedly lacking several important parts of its cultural development. Can it really be the artistic wasteland that so many people claim? After all, it produced Bryan Adams...

Houses of ill-fame in Toronto? Certainly not. The whole city is an immense house of ill-fame.
C.S. Clark, 1826–1909

How utterly destitute of all light and charm are the intellectual conditions of our people and the institutions of our public life! How barren! How barbarous!
Archibald Lampman, 1861–1899, on Canada

Canada is a country without a soul – live, but, unlike the States, not kicking.
Rupert Brooke, 1887–1915

The cold narrow minds, the confined ideas, the bygone prejudices of the society are hardly conceivable; books there are none, nor music, and as to pictures! The Lord deliver us from such! The people do not know what a picture is.
Anna Jameson, 1794–1860

The only poet in Canada was very nice to me in Ottawa. Canada's a bloody place for a sensitive real poet like this to live all his life in.
Rupert Brooke

As false as a diamond from Canada.
French saying

Of course, being so far north, Canada has plenty of that irritating weather to cope with.

Canada has a climate that consists of nine months winter and three months late fall.
American saying

I find that Newfoundland is said to be celebrated for its codfish, its dogs, its hogs, its fogs.
Sir William Whiteway, 1828–1908

A rascally heap of sand, rock and swamp, called Prince Edward Island, in the horrible Gulf of St Lawrence; that lump of worthlessness bears nothing but potatoes.
William Cobbett, 1762–1835

I no longer wonder the elegant arts are unknown here; the rigour of the climate suspends the very powers of the understanding: what then must become of those of the imagination?
Frances Brooke, 1745–1789, on Canada

Good God, what sums the nursing of that ill-troven, hardvisaged and ill-favour brat, Nova Scotia, has cost this nation.
Edmund Burke, 1729–1797

British Columbia is a barren, cold mountain country that is not worth keeping. The place has been going from bad to worse.
Henry Labouchère, 1798–1869

Toronto as a city carries out the idea of Canada as a country. It is a calculated crime both against the aspirations of the soul and the affection of the heart.
Aleister Crowley, 1875–1947

The situation of the town is very unhealthy, for it stands on a piece of low marshy land, which is better calculated for a frog-pond or beaver meadow than for the residence of human beings.
Edward Talbot, 1801–1839, on Toronto

Finally, as if all the previous insults weren't enough to put down a place supposedly not worth putting down, several of the more cruel commentators have seen fit to drag up Canada's historical national divide.

That the two tribes of men, French and English, do not assimilate is no new discovery; it is nothing more than Nature herself did when she deliberately created the English Channel.
Sir Francis Bond Head, 1793–1875, on French and English Canadians

Québec is not a province like the others. She is more stupid.
Gérard Filion, 1891–1976

A sub-arctic lumber village converted by royal mandate into a political cock-fighting pit.
Goldwin Smith, 1823–1910, on Ottawa

This two-cultured, multi-ghettoed, plural community, this non-nation, nay-saying, no-place of an un-Eden, this faceless, unidentifiable blank on the map.
William Killbourn, 1950–

On the other side of the world, Australia and New Zealand have also attracted a lot of negative commentary. Australia, in particular, has never quite lived down its days as an English penal colony, and the Antipodean peoples have a reputation for being blunt, no-nonsense, hard-drinking, and altogether uncouth.

To live in Australia permanently is rather like going to a party and dancing all night with your mother.
Barry Humphries, 1934–

Australia may be the only country in the world in which the word "academic" is regularly used as a term of abuse.
Dame Leonie Kramer, 1925–

So you're going to Australia? What are you going to sing? All I can say is sing 'em muck – it's all they understand.
Dame Nellie Melba, 1861–1931, giving advice to a fellow soprano

The Sydney Opera House looks as if it is something that has crawled out of the sea and is up to no good.
Beverley Nichols, 1898–1983, on Sydney, Australia

Pathological exhibits, human scum, paranoiacs, degenerates, morons, bludgers, packs of dingoes, industrial outlaws and political lepers, ratbags. If these people went to Russia, Stalin wouldn't even use them for manure.
Arthur Calwell, 1896–1996, on communist Australians

I find it hard to say, because when I was there, it seemed to be shut.
Clement Freud, on whether or not he liked New Zealand

Moving back up to Europe, after Britain, one country stands out as the target of international invective. Arrogant, poorly washed, militant, smug, garlic-eating, rude, supercilious, ignorant ... the list of charges goes on and on. The luckless recipient of all this malediction is, of course, France. A land of cheese and wine. A land of sexual liberation and passion. A land of romance. A land which, according to the following people, leaves rather a lot to be desired.

A small acquaintance with history shows that all governments are selfish, and the French governments more selfish than most.
Lord Eccles, 1904–

France was long a despotism tempered by epigrams.
Thomas Carlyle, 1795–1881

He lies like a French bulletin.
Dutch saying

It took no more effort than casting a Frenchman into hell.
Dutch saying

Attila, the scourge of God; the French, his brothers.
Italian saying

A fighting Frenchman runs away from even a she-goat.
Russian saying

France is a country where the money falls apart in your hands and you can't tear the toilet paper.
Billy Wilder, 1906–

The French are particularly well-known for their arrogance and, following on the heels of their promiscuity, they are also known for their spectacular sexual diseases.

Paris is like a whore. From a distance she seems ravishing, you can't wait until you have her in your arms. Five minutes later you feel empty, disgusted with yourself. You feel tricked.
Henry Miller, 1891–1980, on Paris, France

May the French Ulcer love you and the Lord hate you.
Arab curse – the "French ulcer" is syphilis

When the Frenchman sleeps, the devil rocks him.
French saying

French pox and a leather vest last for life.
German saying – "French pox" is syphilis again

The French write other than they speak, and speak other than they mean.
German saying

The friendship of the French is like their wine – exquisite, but of short duration.
German saying

I do not dislike the French from the vulgar antipathy between neighbouring nations, but for their insolent and unfounded airs of superiority.
Horace Walpole, 1717–1797

When they aren't being rude though, the French people are apparently being foolish instead.

The nation is divided into two species: the one of idle monkeys who mock at everything; and the other of tigers, who tear.
Voltaire, 1694–1778, on France

To speak French means to have no sense.
Colonial French saying

How can one conceive of a one-party system in a country that has over two hundred varieties of cheese?
Charles de Gaulle, 1890–1970, on France

They do everything and know nothing.
Italian saying, about the French

They are a short, blue-vested people who carry their own onions when cycling abroad, and have a yard which is 3.37 inches longer than other people's.
Alan Coren, 1938–, on the French

The French do not say what they mean; they do not read as they write; and they do not sing according to the notes.
Italian saying

The ignorance of French society gives one a rough sense of the infinite.
Joseph Renan, 1823–1892

Only a dog or a Frenchman walks after he has eaten.
French saying

Britain has football hooligans, Germany has neo-Nazis, and France has farmers.
The Times newspaper, 1992

Germany is unfortunate enough to have a bad reputation that is the automatic result of being the villain – that is, the losing side – of two huge, devastating wars in less than a hundred years. Try as you might, that's an awful lot of bad publicity to work around. German efficiency is legendary, which might just contribute to the problem. Plenty of people have certainly found plenty of things to pick at.

Two World Wars and one World Cup, doodah, doodah!
English anti-German football taunt, to the tune of *Yankee Doodle*

The German may be a good fellow, but it is best to hang him just the same.
Russian saying

One thing I will say for the Germans – they are always perfectly willing to give somebody's land to somebody else.
Will Rogers, 1879–1935

Marry a German and you'll see that the women have hairy tongues.
Ruthenian saying

When a snake warms himself on ice, a German will begin to wish a Czech well.
Czech saying

Rather die with Denmark than rot with Prussia
Danish saying

Wherever Germans are, it is unhealthy for Italians.
Italian saying

The German lies as soon as he becomes polite.
German saying

Perhaps unsurprisingly, the Germans are characterized as being rather dangerous to trust, a feature which the Polish people seem particularly keen to remind others of.

Better Turkish hatred than German love.
Croatian saying

With the Germans friendship make, but as neighbours do not take.
German saying

The great virtues of the German people have created more evils than idleness ever did vices.
Paul Valéry, 1871–1945

Hungarians, trust the Germans not;
Be their promise ever so hot,
And though they give you a seal
On it as large as a wheel
There is absolutely nothing to it.
Hungarian saying

Peace with the German is like a wolf and a sheep living together.
Polish saying

One German a beer; two Germans an organization; three Germans a war.
Polish saying

Serve a German with all your heart and your reward will be a fart.
Polish saying

The German is as sly as the plague.
Polish saying

God invented man; the Devil invented the German.
Polish saying

German goods are fragile and German words deceptive.
Finnish saying

Like English, the German language is also the target of attack.

Life is too short to learn German.
Richard Porson, 1759–1808

I speak Spanish to God, Italian to women, French to men, and German to my horse.
Holy Roman Emperor Charles V, 1500–1558

At the same time as being cunning and dangerous, the Germans are also supposed by several peoples to be stupid. Exactly how they manage to combine the three is never really made particularly clear.

The East German manages to combine a Teutonic capacity for bureaucracy with a Russian capacity for infinite delay.
Goronwy Rees, 1903–1974

He's like a German.
Lithuanian saying, meaning "He can't understand reason"

The German – as opposed to the human – mind.
William James, 1842–1910

The German may be as big as a poplar tree, but he is as stupid as a bean.
Polish saying

The German mind has a talent for making no mistakes but the very greatest.
Clifton Fadiman, 1904–

A dead German, a dead dog; the difference is but slight.
Polish saying

The German people are fond of their food and drink. Far too fond of them, in fact, if some people are to be believed.

God guard us against the health of the Germans and the malady of the French.
French saying, warning against alcoholism and, yes, syphilis respectively

The Germans gorge and swill themselves to poverty and hell.
German saying

When the Russian steals, he does it that he might have enough for himself for a single day, but when the German steals he takes enough for his children and the morrow.
German saying

Three things are in trouble: birds in the hands of children, young girls in the hands of old men, and wine in the hands of Germans.
Italian saying

How much disgruntled heaviness, lameness, dampness, how much beer is there in the German intelligence.
Friedrich Nietzsche, 1844–1900

The Prussians have two stomachs and no heart.
German saying

A traditional enemy of England, Spain was another country which aggressively built itself a mighty empire, albeit largely by infecting South America with smallpox. Nowadays, it is known negatively for bad food, bad architecture, and bad attitudes. The Costa Del Sol, on the south coast, is particularly famous across Europe for being a place for criminals and karaoke performers to escape justice.

In a Spanish inn, you will find only what you have brought there yourself.
French saying

He who would eat in Spain must bring his kitchen along.
German saying

The only good thing that comes from the east is the sun.
Portugese saying; note that Spain is to the east of Portugal

A country that has sold its soul for cement and petrol, and can only be saved by a series of earthquakes.
Cyril Connolly, 1903–1974

He speaks French like a Spanish cow.
French saying

One of the most hideous buildings in the world.
George Orwell, 1903–1950, on Barcelona Cathedral, Spain

The Spaniard is a bad servant, but a worse master.
English saying

A Spaniard may be trusted – but no further than your nose.
German saying

Spaniards are like lice – once they are there, it is difficult to get rid of them.
German saying

A Spaniard and a braggart are the same thing.
German saying

Italy is a fascinating country with a long, rich history. The Roman Empire swarmed out of it two thousand years ago, give or take a century or three, and took over most of the surrounding area, before plunging Europe into the Dark Ages when it collapsed. Since then, the region has given us the Catholic church, the Mafia, and spaghetti bolognaise. Still, it's a very lovely country, isn't it? Maybe not...

Venice is excessively ugly in the rain – it looks like King's Cross.
Sir John Gielgud, 1904–, on Venice, Italy

If there is a Hell, Rome is built on top of it.
German saying

Venice is like eating an entire box of chocolate liqueurs at one go.
Truman Capote, 1924–1984, on Venice, Italy

Rome reminds me of a man who lives by exhibiting to travellers his grandmother's corpse.
James Joyce, 1882–1941, on Rome, Italy

Italy is paradise for horses and hell for women.
German saying

Italians also have a reputation for being hard to trust. With such eminently plain-talking and honourable people as Emperor Nero, Lucretia Borgia, Machiavelli and Mussolini in its past, it's difficult to imagine where such an impression could come from.

Italian devotion and German fasting have no meaning.
Danish saying

Half an Italian in a house is one too many.
German and French saying

Italian soup.
Czech term for poison

The Italian will kill his father for money.
Greek saying

To cook an egg, to make a bed for a dog, and to teach an Italian to do anything are three hard things.
German saying

Cross yourself once before an Andalusian and thrice on spotting an Italian.
Spanish saying

The Dutch are a rather unusual people by European standards. For one thing, they're generally pleasant to pretty much everyone. They're also practical, open-minded, organized and, for the most part, fairly peaceful. It will come as no surprise then to learn that in the absence of more robust faults, they are also characterized as being somewhat plain to look at, and as dull as ditchwater.

We always like our pop stars to be like Greek gods: bigger, better and uglier than us. We hate the bores, Jesus Christ and the Dutch. Especially the Dutch.
Malcolm McLaren, 1947–

Compared with Greece and Italy, Holland is but a platter-faced, cold-gin-and-water country, after all, and a heavy, barge-built, web-footed

race are its inhabitants.
Sir Francis Bond Head, 1793–1875

Holland is a country where the earth is better than the air; where profit is sought more than humour; where there is more sense than esprit; where there is more goodwill than good humour; where there is more prosperity than humour; and where a visit is preferable to living.
German saying

The Dutch fall into two quite distinct physical types – the small, corpulent, red-faced Edams and then thinner, paler, larger Goudas.
Alan Coren, on the Dutch

Apart from cheese and tulips, the main product of Holland is advocaat, a drink made from lawyers.
Alan Coren, on the Dutch

A dark German, a blond Italian and a red Spaniard seldom mean well, like a Dutchman of any colour.
German saying

How can we secure food when the Dutchman spoils what is good?
German saying

The English eat most, the Germans drink most, while the Dutch eat and drink most of all.
French saying

Another nation infamous for being dull is Switzerland. In many cases, though, the Swiss are worse than the Dutch – after all, they have one of the world's densest populations of bankers...

Since its national products – snow and chocolate – both melt, the cuckoo clock was invented solely in order to give tourists something solid to remember it by.
Alen Coren, on Switzerland

In Italy, for thirty years under the Borgias, they had warfare, terror, murder, bloodshed, and they produced Michelangelo, Leonardo da Vinci and the Renaissance. In Switzerland they had brotherly love, five hundred years of democracy and peace, and what did they produce? The cuckoo clock.
Orson Welles, 1915–1985, on Switzerland, in *The Third Man*

A country to be in for two hours, or two and a half if the weather is fine, and no more. Ennui comes in the third hour, and suicide attacks you before the night.
Lord Brougham, 1778–1868

I don't like Switzerland – it has produced nothing but theologians and waiters.
Oscar Wilde

Switzerland has produced the numbered bank account, Ovaltine and Valium.
Peter Freedman, 1912–

No more money, no more Swiss.
French saying

The Swiss has two bad nights when he can't sleep – one where he has overloaded his stomach, and the other where he is lying awake thinking about how he can overload it again.
German saying

You may as well bang your head into a wall as talk to a Swiss.
French saying

Back down out of the Alps and into the Mediterranean, the Greeks and Cypriots have an entirely different reputation. Treacherous, loud, excitable, unreliable, lazy, dull-witted – but never boring. No way. The Greeks are far too frustrating to be dull.

The Greeks – dirty and impoverished descendants of a bunch of la-de-da fruit salads who invented democracy and then forgot how to use it while walking around dressed up like girls.
P.J. O'Rourke, 1948–

Three Turks and three Greeks make six heathens.
Serbian saying

Realizing they will never be a world power, the Cypriots have decided to settle for being a world nuisance.
George Mikes

In Cyprus, three things are cheap wholesale but expensive retail: salt, sugar and whores.
Greek saying

Few things can be less tempting or less dangerous than a Greek woman of the age of thirty.
John Carne, 1906–1996

A crab is no fish, and a Greek is no man.
Russian saying

Wherever there are people who have had the "fortune" to do business with the Greeks, you seem to find proverbs suggesting that they are wholly dishonest and unreliable. They say there's no smoke without fire.

The Greeks tell the truth, but only once a year.
Russian saying

After shaking hands with a Greek, count your fingers.
Albanian saying

One Greek can outwit ten Jews.
Bulgarian saying

A Russian can be cheated only by a Gypsy; a Gypsy by a Jew; a Jew by a Greek; and a Greek by the Devil.
Greek saying

All Cretans are liars.
Greek saying

Another country where the occupants have been widely criticized for just about everything is Poland. A country with a rather up-and-down history, its occupants have been accused of the majority of all available crimes – including selfishness, dirtiness, dishonesty, weakness, evil, and just plain nastiness.

A Jew thinks first of wife and child; a Pole thinks first of horse and dog.
Yiddish saying

Love without jealousy is like a Pole without lice.
French saying

The Alps divide us from the Italians,
From the French the river separates us,
The sea is between us and the English,
But only hate keeps us and the Poles apart.
German rhyme

Where the women are stronger than the men.
Russian saying, about Poland

The Pole is a thief.
German saying

Why does the devil take the Poles? Because they are glad to go along.
Russian saying

One of the more common recurrent themes is that the Polish are dumb.

The Pole has a large mouth, but there is nothing behind it.
German saying

Where there are three Poles there will be five opinions.
German saying

What an Englishman invents, a Frenchman designs, or a German patches together, a stupid Pole will buy and a Russian take from him.
Polish saying

Rather than being stupid or dirty, as the Poles are supposed to be, the Hungarians are more generally considered to be crooked.

Poles and Czechs are like two close leaves, but when joined by the Hungarian they make three fine thieves.
German saying

Do not trust a Hungarian unless he has a third eye in his forehead.
Czech saying

Where there is a Slav, there is song; where there is a Hungarian, there is rage.
Slovakian saying

Sins are born in Hungary.
Czech saying

As base as a Hungarian.
Polish saying

If the Hungarian attitude towards the Slovaks is any indication of their general opinion of foreigners, perhaps it is no surprise that they have a bad reputation for dishonesty. They seem quite convinced that the Slovaks merit no real consideration as members of humankind.

He is a Slovak; in other words, he is not a person.
Hungarian saying

Potatoes are not food and Slovaks are not human beings.
Hungarian saying

If you invite the Slovak to stay, he may turn you out of your house any day.
Hungarian saying

One of the most maligned groups in Europe are the Gypsies. It seems that no matter where you go, they are looked down upon. They are accused of stealing pots, clothes, cattle, even children. Wherever they stopped, there would be people agitating to get them to move on. It terms of being considered loathsome and contemptible, they are one of the most highly criticized of all peoples. It is interesting that although everyone still remembers the millions of Jews who were murdered in the Nazi Holocaust, far fewer remember the vast numbers of Gypsies who were also killed...

Three people, four horses or five Gypsies.
German saying

When you cut the Gypsy in ten pieces, you have not killed him, you have only made ten Gypsies.
English saying

Where a Jew could not go, the Gypsy crept.
Russian saying

When the Gypsy was made king, the first man he hanged was his father.
Serbian saying

Once in his life a Gypsy tells the truth, but he then repents of it.
Russian saying

He is used to misery like a Gypsy to the gallows.
German saying

The Gypsy has three truths: one with me, one with you, and the third with himself.
Ukrainian saying

Work a little, steal a little, are the rules of Gypsy life.
Serbian saying

Gypsy truth is worse than orthodox lie.
Russian saying

For years, Russia was the big enemy, the bogey with which Western governments used to scare their people. More recently, it has slipped back into the same sort of role in the world that it held before Communism – it's huge, it's cold, it's not particularly civilized, but above all, it's depressing.

Moscow, as I saw it once, is Horrorsville.
James Kirkup, 1923–

Los Angeles without the sun or grass.
Lillian Hellman, 1907–1984 on Moscow

A more lifeless, depressing city does not exist on the face of the planet. Even Siberians call this "The End of the World".
Harry de Windt, 1884–1969, on Yatsuk, Russia

The devil you can ban with the cross, but a Russian you can never get rid of.
Ukrainian saying

A nation of sheep. Angry sheep, but nevertheless sheep, and in sheep's clothing.
James Kirkup

Make ye no truce with Adam-zad, the bear that walks like a man.
Rudyard Kipling, 1865–1936, on Russia

As with most other nations, many people claim that Russians are inherently villainous and dishonest. If all the peoples of earth have the reputation of being dishonest with their neighbours – and with the possible exceptions of the Dutch and the Swiss, most seem to – then maybe this tells us something about humans, and not about specific nationalities?

How can you tell a Russian? Go to sleep and he will rob you.
Ukrainian saying

If a Russian is in the hills, count your olives.
Greek saying

The Russian knows the way, yet he asks for directions.
Ukrainian saying

Better the Devil in your house than a Russian.
Ukrainian saying

The Russian looks like a crow, but he is slyer than the devil.
Ukrainian saying

If a Russian tells you it's dry, put your collar up.
Ukrainian saying

The Tartar sells his own father.
Osmanli saying

Turkey is in a strange position, not knowing whether to claim it is European or Middle-Eastern. Different regimes have had different ideas on which way to jump. At the start of the century, so many people were describing Turkey as "the sick man of Europe" that the cliché even filtered through to the generally impervious brains of leaders all around the world.

The sick old man of Europe.
Kaiser Wilhelm II, 1859–1941

The sick old man of the East.
Tsar Nicholas II, 1868–1918

Before World War I, Turkey was known as the sick man of Europe. Now it is almost terminal.
Richard Nixon, 1909–1983

However, while their rulers were repeating each other, the general public had a different opinion of the Turks. They have generally been seen as cruel, bloodthirsty monsters. Given the terrifying little doner kebab takeaway food stalls that have now penetrated Western Europe, many might well agree. For those readers who have not been exposed to this delight of Turkish cuisine – as served from a greasy little van at midnight after a dozen beers – there's no point trying to describe the experience; just count your blessings, and be grateful that "sheep fat" merely sounds unpleasant. Many cultures have proverbs which claim that after a Turk has passed, the ground is contaminated. But doner kebabs have already been discussed...

As cruel as a Turk.
Greek saying

How will you tell a Turk? By the blood on his hands.
Greek saying

Be at guard with old Turks and young Serbs.
Czech saying

That was too cruel even for a Turk
Dutch saying

Where the Turk treads, for a hundred years the soil bears no fruit.
German saying

No grass grows in the trail of a Turk.
Arab saying

Where the Turk's horse treads once, the grass never grows again.
English saying

As if that wasn't enough, the Turks are also considered to be greedy and uncivilized.

Will they ever be civilized? I think not. Such a fine country ought to be in better hands.
John Webster, 1580–1825, on Turkey

A Turk who hears the word "Paradise" asks "Is there any gold to be looted there?"
Persian saying

No cold without a gust; no bad guest without a Turk.
Serbian saying

Perfectly useless.
Horatio Nelson, 1758–1805, on the Turks

The Arabic-speaking lands of the Middle East have often been considered – and criticized – together. Dirty, fickle, and dishonest, apparently, the Arabs have a fairly bad reputation, all things considered.

I do not wish for camel's milk and I do not wish for the sight of an Arab.
Turkish saying

The Arab takes his bath in vain; he will become no whiter.
Turkish saying

The serpent who seduced Eve spoke Arabic; Adam and Eve made love in Persian; the angel that drove them out of Paradise spoke Turkish.
Turkish saying

The Paradise of Thieves.
Eliza Fry, 1780–1845, on Egypt

I never saw a place I liked worse, nor which afforded less pleasure or instruction, nor antiquities which less answered their description.
James Bruce, 1730–1794, on Egypt

There is not perhaps upon Earth a more dirty metropolis.
E.D. Clarke, 1840 – 1893, on Cairo, Egypt

A practical joke played on history.
Peter Forster, 1818–1886, on the Pyramids of Egypt

The Persian Gulf is the arsehole of the world, and Basra is 80 miles up it.
Harry Hopkins, 1889–1946, on Iran

An artificial Babel.
Henry Tanner, 1859–1937, on Beirut, Lebanon

The inscrutable Orient has baffled and irritated a large number of different people. The dominant cultures of the Far East, China and Japan, have often been greatly misunderstood by Westerners. Even worse are the occasions where they have been understood all too well.

There are only two kinds of Chinese – those who give bribes, and those who take them.
Russian saying

It is like Chinese grammar.
Russian saying, meaning something is incomprehensible

I found the Pearl of the Orient slightly less exciting than a rainy Sunday evening in Rochester.
S.J. Perelman, 1904–1979, on Macao, China

He has Chinese luck.
Spanish saying, meaning that someone has undeserved good fortune

Harbin is now being called the Chicago of the East. This in not a compliment to Chicago.
Maurice Baring, 1944–, on Harbin, China

A kind of low-life Venice of the Orient.
James Kirkup on Keelung, Taiwan

The Japanese have almost as big a reputation for cruelty as do young children.
Dennis Bloodworth, 1718–1780

I don't greatly admire Japanese women; they have no figures to speak of, and look as if a bee had stung them in the eye.
Crosbie Garstin, 1923–1988

A land of disappointments.
American saying, about Japan

Of course, plenty of bad things have been said about just about everywhere. No matter where you go, someone else has been there before, and they didn't much like either the place or the locals. Maybe fewer people have been offensive about Iceland than about England or America, but that shouldn't necessarily be taken to mean that the Icelanders are any more popular – it could just mean that fewer people have come into contact with them. So, in the spirit of bad feeling, here's a generous selection of the best put-downs levelled at the rest of the world to finish up with, starting with Europe.

Take from a Spaniard all his good qualities and there remains a Portuguese.
Spanish saying

Beer is the Danish national drink, and the Danish national weakness is another beer.
Clementine Paddleford, 1898–1967

I see nothing here but ruins.
Mary Wollstonecraft, 1759–1797, on Denmark

Finland is the devil's country.
Russian saying

About as exciting as Aberdeen on a Sunday night.
Anon, on Reykjavik, Iceland

Bold as an Iceland lion.
Danish saying; by "Iceland lion", they mean a sheep, the Icelanders supposedly being cowardly

That isn't a dog – that's a Fleming.
Walloon saying. Flemings and Walloons are the two groups which make up Belgium

It's the sort of place you get into as late as possible, bring your own food, go to bed, get up, go for a walk, play the game and get out.
Jack Charlton, 1935–, on Albania

To identify a Romanian, show him a wallet and ask him who it belongs to.
Russian saying

"What a stupid lot these Germans are," says the Czech. "I have been here 10 years, and they still can't understand me."
German saying

One Jew can cheat ten Germans, one Greek can cheat ten Jews, and one Armenian can cheat ten Greeks.
German saying

It takes three Jews to cheat a Greek, three Greeks to cheat a Syrian, and three Syrians to cheat an Armenian.
Arabic saying

Africa has had fewer insults hurled at it by Europe and America than many other regions. Then again, there's no real need to be rude about a continent that you have marched into, conquered, stripped the best of the natural resources from, and dragged the people away from in chains as slaves. After all, what insult could possibly match that? Well, some people have given it a spirited go.

"Diarrhoea City", oh fuck yes, terrible place. You don't even have to eat anything for that. It's the dust from the camel shit. One of the worst places I've ever been.
Michael Caine, 1933–, on Ouazazate, Morocco

The name, which means "my joy" in Amharic, seems peculiarly inappropriate.
Paul Henze, 1926–, on Dessie, Ethiopia

The less said about Massawa the better. It was one of those dark patches that are best forgotten.
Geoffrey Harmsworth, 1865–1922, on Massawa, Ethiopia

The desert of Danakil is a part of the world that the Creator must have fashioned when He was in a bad mood.
Ladislas Farago, 1791–1867, on Ethiopia

It looks as if it has been dropped, piecemeal, from an aeroplane carrying rubbish.
John Gunther, 1881–1926, on Addis Ababa, Ethiopia

If there is any place where love is dead, it is here.
Mary Benson, 1826–1925, on South Africa

Asia, in comparison to Africa, has attracted a fair amount of the wrong kind of attention.

The definition of obscenity.
Geoffrey Moorhouse, 1931–, on Calcutta, India

The Indian wears seven veils which must be removed if his true face is to be seen.
English saying, on India

Delhi is the capital of the losing streak. It is the metropolis of the crossed wire, the missed appointment, the puncture, the wrong number.
Jan Morris, 1949–, on Delhi, India

Trust a Brahman before a snake, and a snake before a harlot, and a harlot before an Afghan.
Hindu saying

I have lived for 78 years without hearing of bloody places like Cambodia.
Sir Winston Churchill, 1874–1965

Outer Mongolia is such a terra incognita that Tibet is practically Coney Island by comparison.
James Gunther, 1901–1970

Finally, despite the vast volume of invective aimed at North America and Canada, some few people have selflessly made time to be rude about other parts of the Americas.

It seemed a cruel, towering place, like an eagle's nest now inhabited by vultures and their dying prey.
Paul Theroux, 1941–, on Bogotá, Colombia

The world's arsehole.
Anon, on Mexico city

The only good Indian is a dead Indian.
American saying, on American Indians

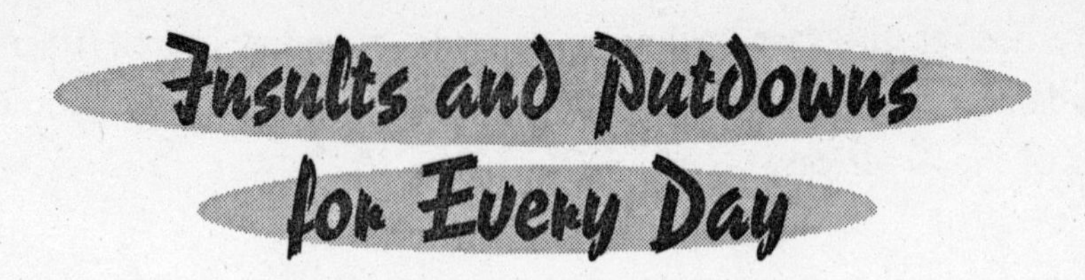

Insults and Putdowns for Every Day

Hah, what a sad collection of droolers. They can't even control their own bladders.
Dave Allsop, 1968–, *SLA Industries*, on junkies

There comes a time in every person's life, no matter how pleasant and patient they are, when they find themselves overwhelmed with the emotional need to say something rude about someone else. It's a perfectly natural reaction to having to deal with someone who is making things unnecessarily difficult for you in one way or another. For many humans, it's a simple reaction to coming into contact with someone else – people like stand-up comedians, New York waiters, train attendants and telephone sales assistants all seem to be perpetually afflicted by the need to be witty and cutting about the folks around them. For the rest of us, being evil-minded is less automatic, and on those occasions when we do want a cutting put-down it often takes us so long to think of one that it's too late to use it. The French, masters of the offensive, have a special name for this phenomenon – *esprit d'escalier*, the humour of the stairs, because your witty reply comes to you as you're half-way down the stairs and on your way out. This chapter will help provide you with the inspiration that you need to be acidically funny in daily life. Insults about film stars and politicians are fascinating, but there are few of us who actually come into contact with these types on a regular basis, and the happier we are for it too, I suspect. The things that do go to make up our regular existence are all criticized here, in this chapter. Everything from family, friends and lovers through to restaurants and lawyers is slated here for you. Next time you want to be actively cruel about anchovies, turkey or cottage cheese – and if you think about it, I'm sure you'll agree that they are all worthy targets for scorn – the inspiration will be here, at your fingertips.

A word of caution, however. The art of being creatively insulting is not the same as being rude and abusive. Anyone can be rude and abusive, and cause offence, quite easily. Sentences like "Why don't you f*** off and f*** your mother up the arse like I did last night, you pathetic, snivelling little piece of s***" are guaranteed to offend just about everyone. They also stand a fairly good chance of getting you into a fight. If you are going to go around being offensive, pick targets with a sense of humour, and deliver your lines in the sort of throw-away, witty manner that makes it fairly plain you are looking to amuse the people around you. If you go for an intense, venomous style that screams "I am attacking you personally", you'll be risking serious consequences. It's all in the delivery...

With that in mind, we're going to start this chapter with a section of personal insults. The authors of these put-downs are all anonymous; in some cases, the lines may have originally come from films or books, while in others, they have been a part of popular culture for years, maybe even for centuries. Of course, no line is truly anonymous – someone, at some time, has said each of them – but finding an original attribution is horribly tangled. These lines can be tailored to fit almost any situation. Some of them refer to male or female targets, but that is largely accidental. They will all fit both men and women – and often they fit like a glove. The most popular target to start with in personal criticism has always been intelligence. By suggesting that your victim is stupid, you're opening hostilities in the most time-honoured way. The following list of crushing put-downs will all make your opponent seem hopelessly lacking in the brain department.

A sharp tongue does not mean that you have a keen mind.

Are you always this stupid, or are you making a special effort today?

Brains aren't everything. In fact, in your case they're nothing!

Don't let your mind wander — it's far too little to be let out on its own.

He always finds himself lost in thought – it's an unfamiliar territory.

He does the work of three men: Larry, Curly and Moe.

He doesn't know the meaning of the word "fear" – but then again he doesn't know the meaning of most words.

I don't know what makes you so dumb, but it really works!

I don't think you are a fool. But what's my opinion compared to that of thousands of others?

I know you are nobody's fool, but maybe someone will adopt you one day.

I would ask you how old you are, but I reckon you can't count that high.

I would have liked to insult you, but the sad truth is that you wouldn't understand me.

If what you don't know can't hurt you, she's practically invulnerable.

If you were twice as smart as you are now, you'd still be absolutely stupid.

I'm blonde. What's your excuse?

I'm glad to see you're not letting your education get in the way of your ignorance.

She has reached rock bottom and shows signs of starting to dig.

Sit down, give your mind a rest – it obviously needs it.

Some drink from the fountain of knowledge, but it looks like this guy just gargled.

Some folks are so dumb, they have to be watered twice a week.

That man is cruelly depriving a village somewhere of an idiot.

What he is lacking in intelligence, he more than makes up for in stupidity.

When I look into your eyes, I see straight through to the back of your head.

Whom am I calling "stupid"? Good question. I don't know. What is your name?

Your mind isn't so much twisted as badly sprained.

Your verbosity is exceeded only by your total stupidity.

Another extremely popular line of attack when being nasty about others is to pick on their looks. There are very few people out there so truly beautiful that their appearance is flawless; for everyone else, there will be something to poke fun at. Looks also have the advantage of being a target that can undermine your victim's confidence for long enough to let you make a quick escape if things look like turning nasty.

I'll bet he opens his post with that nose!

I don't want you to turn the other cheek – it's just as ugly.

Is that your nose, or are you eating a banana?

The next time you shave, could you stand an inch or two closer to the razor please?

This person is without doubt the worst-dressed sentient being in the known universe.

Can I borrow your face for a few days? My ass is going on holiday.

She's so ugly, when she was a little girl, they had to put a pot roast in her lap so the dog would play with her. What a shame the mutt got carried away! Still, the chewed-up look is in this season.

How can you love nature, when it did that to you?

Hey, don't you need a licence to be that ugly?

Every girl has the right to be ugly, but I'm afraid you've abused the privilege.

See, that's what's meant by dark and handsome. When it's dark, he's handsome.

I feel sorry for you because you are so ugly, but I feel even sorrier for myself because I have to look at you.

If I had a face like yours, I'd sue my parents for libel.

If I were as ugly as he is, I wouldn't say hello to people, I'd say boo!

I've hated your looks from the very start they gave me.

I've seen people like you before – but I had to pay admission!

People clap when they see you ... but they clap their hands over their eyes.

Whooey! When he fell out of the ugly tree, boy did he hit every branch on the way down.

You have a face only a mother could love – and even she hates it!

In fact, he has the perfect weapon against muggers – his face!

You're so ugly when you went to the haunted house, they offered you a job.

You're so ugly, you almost look like your mother did, before the operation.

Yours is a prima facie *case of ugliness. Your body is damned ugly, too.*

Being overweight is a sad and depressing thing. The reasons behind it are always complex, and often related to genetic disposition. It doesn't say anything about a person's mental, moral or emotional worth; in fact, many of the heavier people are uncommonly considerate and kind. On the other hand, it is blindingly obvious when someone is fat, and it's almost guaranteed to be a fact that depresses them, which makes it a wonderful target to attack when you want to put someone chubby in their place.

Fat? You're not fat, you're just ... oh, hell, OK. You are fat. Very fat indeed, in fact.

She's so fat, she has the only car in town with stretch marks.

Hey, I remember you when you only had the one stomach.

She's got more chins than the Hong Kong telephone book.

He's so ugly, the robbers gave him their masks to wear.

You don't sweat much for such a fat guy.

I see you were so impressed with your first chin that you added two more.

You're so fat that when you jumped up, you got stuck.

If you really want to upset someone, insult their parentage. It works every time. Put-downs suggesting that your victim is sub-human, non-human or disturbingly inbred can be extremely effective, not to mention extremely offensive. This is one of those topics that you need to treat with a certain degree of care, however. Many people react rather violently to any slur which touches their mother, so you might want to make sure your target has a certain sense of humour before using this particular group of slanders.

After meeting you, I've decided I am in favour of abortion in cases of incestuous rape.

Your ancestors must number in the thousands. It's really hard to understand how so many people can be to blame for producing something like you.

All that you are, you owe to your parents. Why don't you send them some used toilet-roll and get back in credit with them?

Your parents are siblings, right?

You should learn from your parents' mistakes – get sterilized now!

The inbreeding is certainly obvious in your family.

You were born because your mother didn't believe in abortion – and now she believes in infanticide.

It's good to see you're here with your charming sister-cousin-mother-wife, Billy-Jo.

The terrifying power of the human sex drive is horrifically demonstrated by the fact that someone was willing to father you.

Hey, weren't you the poster child for birth control?

You were the answer to a prayer. Your parents prayed that the world would be made to suffer, and you came along.

I bet your mother's bark is worse than her bite!

Tell me, did your parents have any children that lived?

Any similarity between you and a human is purely coincidental.

As an outsider, what do you think of the human race?

Ever since I saw you in your family tree, I've wanted to cut it down.

She'd steal the straw from her mother's kennel.

Hi! I'm a human! What are you?

I heard you were born on a farm. Any more in the litter?

I heard somewhere that your brother was an only child. Now I see it's true

When you were born, God admitted that even He could make a dreadful mistake.

Of course, one of the most common reasons for wanting to be rude to someone is because they're being obnoxious, arrogant, boring, or all three. There are few things in life less bearable than an dull, opinionated windbag sounding off on some topic he or she plainly knows nothing about. The urge to leap up and throttle the person to death is perhaps better expressed as one of the following cutting put-downs:

You are not obnoxious like so many other people – you are obnoxious in a completely different and far worse way.

Grasp your ears firmly and pull; you might just be able to remove your head from your ass.

I don't mind you talking so much, as long as you don't mind me not listening.

Before you came along we were hungry. Now we are fed up.

Don't feel bad – a lot of people have no talent, and you're most of them!

I'd like to see things from your point of view, but I can't seem to get my head that far up your ass.

Do you want me to accept you as you are, or do you want me to lie to myself and try to like you?

Don't you realize that there are enough people to hate in the world already, without your putting in so much effort to give us another?

He has depth, but only on the surface. Deep down inside, he is shallow.

Look here – it's the tall, dark and obnoxious stranger, and is this one ever strange!

I like you. People say I've got no taste, but I like you.

Why don't you go to the library and brush up on your ignorance?

You are such a smart-arse, I bet you could sit on a tub of ice cream and tell me what flavour it is.

If I want any shit from you, I'll squeeze your head.

Please, keep talking. I always yawn when I'm interested.

Breathe the other way, please. Your opinions are bleaching my hair.

There are several people in this world that I find unbearably obnoxious, and you are all of them.

You are so dishonest, I can't even be sure that what you tell me are lies!

I've come across rotting bodies that are less offensive than you are.

You are the kind of person who, when someone first meets you, they don't like you. But when they get to know you better, they hate you.

You have a nasty speech impediment ... your foot.

You must have a low opinion of people, if you think they are your equal.

You used to be arrogant and obnoxious. Now I see that you are just the opposite – you are obnoxious and arrogant.

You've got your head so far up your ass you can chew your food again on the way down.

I hear you changed your mind at last! What did you do with the diaper?

Sometimes, the most effective put-downs are not actually specifically targeting your victim, but instead are bouncing off you as the speaker. In other words, rather than criticizing any specific thing about them, you are criticizing their effect on you, or your opinion of them. That sounds a bit tangled and complicated, but in fact it's really rather obvious – just read through the following set of insults, and the concept of impersonal insults will come clear for you. These lines are wonderfully versatile, as they don't actually rely on any special or specific aspect of the victim. Your hapless opponent doesn't have to be dumb, or fat, or rude; he or she just has to be in hearing range.

I'm busy now. Can I ignore you some other time?

Do you have to leave so soon? I've just poisoned some tea for you.

Pardon me, but you're obviously mistaking me for someone who gives a damn.

I worship the ground that awaits your corpse.

You're a habit I'd like to kick – with both feet.

I've had many cases of love that were just infatuation, but the hate that I feel for you is the real thing.

You remind me of the ocean – you make me sick.

I'd like to give you a going-away present... First, you do your part.

Don't thank me for insulting you – it was a pleasure.

You're not yourself today. I noticed the improvement immediately.

I know you couldn't live without me, so I'll pay for the funeral.

Well, I'll see you in my dreams – if I eat too much cheese.

I used to think that you were a colossal pain in the neck. Now I have a much lower opinion of you.

You are not even beneath my contempt.

I don't want to make a monkey out of you. Why should I take all the credit for the one thing you've done yourself?

I thought of you today. I was at the zoo.

Someone said you were not fit to fuck pigs the other day. I stuck up for you, though. I told them you were.

I will defend, to your death, my right to my opinion.

The final group of personal insults cover all sorts of other aspects that may be ripe for picking on when you find yourself in a war of words. The following batch of slanders don't really fit into any of the previous categories. Whoever it is you want to be unpleasant about, you'll find the perfect put-down here. There's a little something in here for everyone, no matter how hard they try to escape it.

You grow on people... But so does cancer.

If shit was music, you'd be an orchestra.

You should do some soul-searching. You might just find one.

He is so short that when it rains, he is always the last to know.

You really are as pretty as a picture. I know I'd love to hang you.

He's so short, he'd be out of his depth in a parking lot puddle.

Anyone who told you to be yourself couldn't have given you any worse advice.

There are only two things I dislike about her – her faces.

Would you like some cheese to go with that whine?

I can tell that you are lying – your lips are moving.

This is an excellent time for you to become a missing person.

She's the first in her family born without a tail.

You have an inferiority complex – and it's fully justified.

If we killed everybody who hates you, it wouldn't be murder – it would be an apocalypse!

Make somebody happy. Mind your own business.

Ordinarily people live and learn, but you, you just live.

You are not as bad as people say – you are much, much worse.

Her origins are so low, you'd have to limbo under her family tree.

I know you always have your ear to the ground. How's life in the gutter?

Talk is cheap, but that's OK – so are you.

You are living proof that manure can sprout legs and walk.

Her mouth is dirtier than a rubber toilet seat.

He's better at sex than anyone. Now all he needs is a partner.

You would never be able to live down to your reputation, but I see you're doing your best.

You're the best at all you do – and all you do is make people hate you.

She has more faces than Mount Rushmore.

People would follow him anywhere ... but only out of morbid curiosity.

His personality's split so many ways, he goes for group therapy on his own.

If truth is stranger than fiction, then you must be truth!

If sex were fast food, you'd have an M-shaped arch over your head.

Whatever it is that is eating you, it must be suffering horribly.

When you're trying to have a quiet drink in a bar, the chances are the last thing you want is some drunk joker who has mistaken himself – let's face it, it's nearly always going to be a guy hitting on a gal – for Casanova coming over and trying to be impressive. In fact, all he'll manage to do is be intrusive. When you are the victim of unwanted attention, it's best to make things absolutely clear from the start. If you can do so in a loud and disdainful tone of voice, you might even be able to discourage other lecherous jokers from stumbling over to you and being unnecessarily smarmy. Although most young male readers are, at this point, cursing this section, there are advantages to it for the chatter-up, too. Firstly, you'll know immediately if the woman you're pursuing is totally uninterested, and secondly, you'll have an idea what rejection she might throw at you. If you take the time to think up some witty deflections for the negative response to whichever chat-up line you favour, you'll seem doubly impressive. So, in fact, this section is practically a public service...!

Man: *I'd like to call you. What's your number?*
Woman: *It's in the phone book.*
Man: *But I don't know your name.*
Woman: *That's in the phone book too.*

Man: *Haven't we met before?*
Woman: *Yes, I'm one of the nurses at the VD clinic.*

Man: *I'd go through anything for you.*
Woman: *Good! Let's start with your bank account and credit cards.*

Man: *Haven't I seen you somewhere before?*
Woman: *Yeah, that's why I don't go there any more.*

Man: *Is this seat empty?*
Woman: *Yes, and this one will be too if you sit down.*

Man:	*What's a nice girl like you doing in a place like this?*
Woman:	*Waiting for some idiot like you to come along and bore me to tears with pathetic lines.*

Man:	*Your place or mine?*
Woman:	*Both. You're going to yours, and I'm going to mine.*

Man:	*So what do you do for a living?*
Woman:	*I'm a female impersonator.*

Man:	*Hey, come on baby, we're both here at this bar for the same reason.*
Woman:	*Yeah! Let's pick up some chicks!*

Man:	*Hey, baby, what's your sign?*
Woman:	*No Parking.*
or	*Danger of Death.*
or	*No Entry.*

Man:	*How do you like your eggs in the morning?*
Woman:	*Unfertilized.*

Man:	*So, d'ya wanna go back to my place?*
Woman:	*Well, I don't know. Will two people fit under a rock?*

Man:	*Can I buy you a drink?*
Woman:	*Thanks, I'll have a case of champagne. Leave it at the bar for me and I'll pick it up later.*

Man:	*I'm here to fulfil your every sexual fantasy.*
Woman:	*You mean you can lend me a donkey and a great dane?*
Man:	*Your body is like a temple.*
Woman:	*There are no services today.*
Man:	*If I could see you naked, I'd die happy.*
Woman:	*Yeah, but if I saw* you *naked, I'd die laughing.*
Man:	*I would go to the end of the world for you.*
Woman:	*Wonderful! Will you stay there, too?*
Man:	*I know how to please a woman.*
Woman:	*Then please leave me alone.*
Man:	*I want to give myself to you.*
Woman:	*Sorry, I don't accept cheap, nasty gifts.*
Man:	*I can tell that you want me.*
Woman:	*You're so right. I want you to go away.*
Man:	*Hey babe, how 'bout you and I hitting the hot spots?*
Woman:	*Sorry, I don't date outside my species.*

Sometimes, you'll find yourself on the receiving end of an insult or put-down. You might have just been slapped with one of the pick-up rejections above. Your opponent might even have made some unpleasant comment in response to an insult of your own. This sort of person should be thought of, and treated, just like a heckler at a comedy show – because, let's face it, comedians get more insults than almost anyone else. When you get into a battle of wits, it's good to think of it as comedy, because the more passers-by you can get in on your side, the better your position, plus you get a reputation for being stylish. A contest of witty put-downs often turns into a form of competitive performance comedy, with the winner being the one who gets the most laughs. Alternatively, you may actually be an entertainer by trade. Either way, these hints for dealing with hecklers will come in useful. Professional entertainers are well used to members of the audience throwing sarcasm, abuse and even blunt objects at them. The general public can be a very harsh critic, so most comedians have a big store of put-downs waiting for anyone brave or foolish enough to make themselves a target. The comedian will lose face with the audience if the heckler is not dealt with effectively, so often the first concern is to get the dissenter to be quiet.

On a scale of 1 to 10, shut up.

Unless you have something funny to say, shut your face.

Oh my, I am amused. I bet you're really pleased you crawled out of your hole to say that.

Little girls should be seen and not heard.
This requires that the heckler is male; if female, say *boys* instead of *girls.*

...and that, ladies and gentlemen, is the difference between a comedian and an asshole – about 15 feet.

An alternative approach is to be personally offensive to the heckler. Suggesting that he or she is drunk, stoned or stupid is always popular, as are attacks on maturity, sexuality and appearance.

I'll let you off. I remember the first time I tried beer.

You're quite cute. What can I get for a twenty?

The anonymous alcoholic, ladies and gentlemen!

I'm impressed; I've never met such a small mind inside such a big head before.

Congratulations; you're a perfect argument against brother-sister marriages.

That can't be your face. Did your neck throw up?

Ick. What a disgusting slob. Somebody call security; we've been invaded by killer slugs.

Hey, I didn't know you could get epilepsy without a brain.

You've heard about the good time had by all, ladies and gentlemen – and here she is.

In common with much of the world, comedians often like to be offensive about a heckler's family. Mothers are a favourite line of attack in any situation where acidic comments are warranted. There's something very personal about having your mother insulted. It is one of the gambits that is most likely to result in violence however, so budding performers might like to treat the subject with a degree of caution. For the brave or reckless, however, dear old ma is a source of endless inspiration.

You know, your mother is really good in bed – but I guess you found that out for yourself already.

This may look easy to you, but I assure you your mother is even easier.

When you were born, did they let your mother out of her cell?

I heard your mother had an abortion, and now I see it's true.

I went to the ice cream parlour round the corner, and the special of the day was your mother. I had three scoops, in a cone.

That's a low blow – and talking of low blows, how's your mother?

Tell me, how many Peeping Toms has your mother cured?

Youth is no protection. It takes a slightly subtler touch to deal with unruly children in an audience, but there's still plenty of room for genuine venom. Circumstances vary, of course. An entertainer hired to perform at a children's party may find that anything other than amused tolerance puts their fee at risk. In contrast, an obtrusive young person in the audience of a show that is supposed to be adults-only is fair game for whatever twisted epithets end up flying their way.

What's wrong, don't you get any attention back home?

Look folks – a face not even a mother could love.

Now we know why some animals eat their own children.

What do you want to do if you grow up?

I have a child's soul – in a special jar back home.

I bet you get bullied a lot.

Say, you're really special, aren't you.

One final area of popular attack is social status – the comedian implies that the heckler comes from a bad part of town, or works in an unpleasant, menial or sexual job. Unfashionable hobbies and interests can also be suggested to belittle the victim.

Look, this is my job. I don't turn up at your work and spit on the burgers.

Let me guess – tonight's square dance was cancelled, right?

Excuse me, I'm trying to work here. How would you like it if I started yelling down the alley while you're giving blow-jobs to transsexuals?

Where are you from? I'm sorry? No, I heard OK; I just pity you.

Moving on from the art of personal criticism, it is time to look at the rest of life. One of the most pervasive aspects of existence, one of the things that we talk about, dream about, and long for, more than almost anything other than money, is true love. The joy of being with someone who you adore and who you know adores you back is almost unparalleled – according to rumour. And therein lies the trouble. Love is a wondrous thing, but it seems to be just about as elusive as moonbeams and tax rebates. Few people have genuinely experienced true love; far fewer still have had it last for any length of time. Just imagine, all those people, men and women, all across the globe, desperately yearning for someone to love and be loved by and not finding anyone, despite the fact that everyone around them feels the same. Depressing, isn't it?

True love is like ghosts, which everyone talks about, but very few have seen.
François de la Rochefoucalt, 1613–1680

There is only one way to be happy by means of the heart – to have none.
Paul Bourget, 1852–1935

The person who loves believes the impossible.
Elizabeth Browning, 1806–1861

My love is like a red, red rose – expensive, and hard to handle.
Anonymous

Love is like measles – all the worse when it comes late in life.
Douglas Jerrold, 1803–1857

Love is not really blind – the bandage is never so tight but that it can peep.
Elbert Hubbard, 1856–1915

Love is the victim's response to the rapist.
Ti-Grace Atkinson, 1956–

Of course it's possible to love a human being – if you don't know them too well.
Charles Bukowski, 1920–1994

Love is like cheap wine – it leads you to the stars, but leaves you with the gutrot of tomorrow.
Chris Garratt, 1933– and Mick Kidd, 1915–1982

Love, love, love – all the wretched cant of it, masking egotism, lust, masochism, fantasy under a mythology of sentimental postures, a welter of self-induced miseries and joys, blinding and masking the essential personalities in the frozen gestures of courtship, in the kissing and the dating and the desire, the compliments and the quarrels which vivify its barrenness.
Germaine Greer, 1939–

I can understand companionship. I can understand bought sex in the afternoon. I cannot understand the love affair.
Gore Vidal, 1925–

Love is only a dirty trick played on us to assure the continuation of the species.
Somerset Maugham, 1874–1965

Women are well aware that what is commonly called sublime and poetical love depends not upon moral qualities, but on frequent meetings, the style in which the hair is done up, and on the colour and cut of the dress.
Leo Tolstoy, 1828–1910

Love may be unattainable, but sex is far more down to earth. After all, everyone's at it all the time – at least, that's the case if you listen to the folks without much in the way of a sex life. Still, sex does happen, in sufficiently vast quantities to ensure that the population of the earth is still expanding. All those babies ... that means sex, that does. So, even if you yourself aren't getting any, there's still a lot of it around. Given the overwhelming majority of people who are less than happy in their daily lives, and the amount of sex that is taking place, it seems fairly obvious that there is a big overlap between people having regular sex and unhappy people. Which means that – unlikely as it may sound to people feeling sexually deprived – having sex does not make you any happier, or make your life any better...

The pleasure is momentary, the position ridiculous, and the price damnable.
Earl of Chesterfield, 1694–1773

It was like kissing the Berlin Wall
Helena Bonham Carter, 1966– , on kissing Woody Allen

The big mistake men make is that when they turn thirteen or fourteen and all of a sudden they've reached puberty they believe that they like women. Actually, you're just horny. It doesn't mean you like women any more at 21 than you did at ten.
Jules Feiffer, 1929–

Two minutes of gooey near-satisfaction followed by weeks of haunting guilt is so much more easily attained at Haagen-Dazs.
Florence Campbell, 1965–

That gentlemen prefer blondes is due to the fact that, apparently, pale hair, delicate skin and an infantile expression represent the very apex of a frailty which every man longs to violate.
Alexander King, 1972–

Foreplay is like beefburgers – three minutes each side.
Victoria Wood, 1957–

Show me a genuine case of platonic friendship, and I will show you two old or homely faces.
Austin O'Malley, 1858–1953

Despite a lifetime of service to the cause of sexual liberation, I have never caught a venereal disease, which makes me feel rather like an Arctic explorer who has never had frostbite.
Germaine Greer

In adolescence, pornography is a substitute for sex, whereas in adulthood sex is a substitute for pornography.
Edmund White, 1940–

Sex at 93 is like playing billiards with a rope.
George Burns, 1896–1997

New coil inserted. Recall Edward II disembowelled at Berkeley Castle.
Sue Limb, 1946–, *Dulce Domum's Bad Housekeeping,* on contraception

There comes a moment in the day when you have written your pages in the morning, attended to your correspondence in the afternoon, and have nothing further to do. Then comes that hour when you are bored; that's the time for sex.
H.G. Wells, 1866–1946

My husband and I had our best sex during our divorce. It was like cheating on our lawyers.
Priscilla Lopez, 1948– , in *Cheaper to Keep Her*

It is important to remember that society's accepted substitute for love and sex is marriage. Don't be fooled. Marriage is not a way of ensuring that you get affection, companionship, and regular sex; it's a way of teaming you up with someone so that, between you, you can afford to pay for the growth and education of ungrateful children. Getting married because you are lonely and sexually deprived is no more sensible than sewing your mouth shut because you're hungry. Married people generally advise unmarried people not to make the same mistake. Unmarried people usually assume that means marriage is actually rather good, and the married people are trying to keep it a secret. Divorce statistics – and over two-thirds of marriages in some areas will end in divorce – suggest the opposite; when married people advise the unmarried to stay well clear, they're being absolutely sincere. Why spoil a good relationship?

The pain of death is nothing compared to the pain of sharing a coffee-pot with a peevish woman.
John Cheever, 1912–1982, on married life

Marriage is like a cage; one sees the birds outside desperately trying to get in, and those inside equally desperate to get out.
Michel de Montaigne, 1533–1592

One was never married, and that's his hell; another is, and that's his plague.
Robert Burton, 1577–1640

Marriage is like the Middle East – there's no solution.
Anonymous

Marriage is a great institution, but I'm not ready to be institutionalized yet.
Mae West, 1892–1980

Marriage is popular because it combines the maximum of temptation with the maximum of opportunity.
George Bernard Shaw, 1856–1950

The greatest sacrifice in married life is the sacrifice of the adventurous attitude towards life.
George Bernard Shaw

When a man marries, dies or turns Hindu, his best friends hear no more of him.
Percy Bysshe Shelly, 1792–1822

When a girl marries, she exchanges the attentions of many men for the inattention of one.
Helen Rowland, 1875–1950

Before marriage, a man will lie awake thinking about something you said. After marriage, he'll fall asleep before you finish saying it.
Helen Rowland

The most difficult year of marriage is the one you're in.
Franklin P. Jones, 1887–1929

Venus, a beautiful, good-natured lady, was the goddess of love; Juno, a terrible shrew, was the goddess of marriage – and they were always mortal enemies.
Jonathan Swift, 1667–1745

Many a man in love with a dimple makes the mistake of marrying the whole girl.
Stephen Leacock, 1869–1944

Marriage is a dull meal with the desert at the beginning.
Henri de Toulouse-Lautrec, 1864–1901

Keep your eyes wide open before marriage, and wide open afterwards.
Ben Franklin, 1706–1790

Marriage always demands the greatest understanding of the art of insincerity possible between two human beings.
Vicki Baum, 1888–1968

If we take matrimony at its lowest, we regard it as no more than a sort of friendship recognized by the police.
Robert Louis Stevenson, 1850–1894

Marriage is give and take. You'd better give it to her, or she'll take it anyway.
Joey Adams, 1971–

Wedding, n: a ceremony in which two persons undertake to become one, one undertakes to become nothing, and nothing undertakes to become supportable.
Ambrose Bierce, 1842–1914, *The Devil's Dictionary*

If you are afraid of loneliness, do not marry.
Anton Chekov, 1860–1904

Marriage is a good deal like a circus – there is not as much in it as represented in the advertising.
Edgar Watson Howe, 1853–1937

When a man marries, it is no more than a sign that the feminine talent for persuasion and intimidation has forced him into a more-or-less abhorrent compromise between his own honest inclinations and best interests.
H.L. Mencken, 1880–1956

When you're bored with yourself, marry, and be bored with someone else.
David Pryce-Jones, 1947–

Marriage is a desperate thing. The frogs in Aesop were extremely wise; they had a great mind to have some water, but they would not leap into the well, because they could not get out again.
John Selden, 1584–1654

Advice to person's about to marry – don't.
Punch magazine, 1845

If, despite all the above advice, you do choose to get married, that means that you will end up with a husband or a wife of some sort. One poorly kept secret is that spouses are just like everybody else, only worse...

I know many married men, I even know a few happily married men, but I don't know one who wouldn't fall down the first open coal-hole running after the first pretty girl who gave him a wink.
George Jean Nathan, 1882–1958

A man being rich is like a girl being pretty. You might not marry her just because she's pretty, but goodness, doesn't it help?
Marilyn Monroe, 1926–1962, in *Gentlemen Prefer Blondes*

There you are, you see; quite simply, if you cannot have your dear husband for a comfort and a delight, for a breadwinner and a crosspatch, for a sofa, a chair or a hot water bottle, one can use him as a cross to be borne.
Stevie Smith, 1902–1971

The majority of husbands remind me of an orang-utan trying to play the violin.
Honoré de Balzac, 1799–1850

The only solid and lasting peace between a man and his wife is, doubtless, a separation.
Earl of Chesterfield, 1694–1773

A man does not have to be a bigamist to have one wife too many.
The Farmer's Almanac magazine, 1966

When a man steals your wife, there is no better revenge than to let him keep her.
Sacha Guitry, 1885–1957

It goes far toward reconciling me to being a woman when I reflect I am thus in no danger of marrying one.
Lady Mary Montagu, 1689–1762

The end result of all that sex and marriage floating around all over the place is birth, of course. Birth hurts. It's something that men cannot really understand, and in general they're extremely grateful for the fact. There are alternatives, but having your stomach hacked open with a sharp knife has never really been all that popular with women, for some reason...

My female friends had told me that giving birth was like shitting a water melon. They lied. It's like excreting a block of flats – complete with patios,

awnings, clothes-lines, television aerials, satellite dishes, backyard barbecues, kidney-shaped swimming pools, gazebos and double garage extensions with the cars parked outside.
Kathy Lette, 1954–, *Foetal Attraction*

Having a baby is like watching two very inefficient removal men trying to get a very large sofa through a very small doorway, only in this case you can't say, "Oh sod it, bring it through the French windows."
Victoria Wood

Giving birth is like sitting on top of the Eiffel Tower and spinning.
Ruby Wax, 1953–

Real mothers think sex is like full-time employment – it's a nice idea, but it'll never happen again in their lifetime.
Victoria Wood

Even the family members and relatives that you aren't married to are likely to prove themselves at least as much of a burden as a blessing. What's worse is that you don't get a chance to choose your parents...

They fuck you up, your mum and dad,
They may not mean to, but they do.
They give you all the faults they had,
And add some extra, just for you.
Philip Larkin, 1922–1986

When you're the only pea in the pod, your parents are likely to get you confused with the Hope Diamond.
Russell Baker, 1925

Children begin by loving their parents. After a time they judge them. Rarely, if ever, do they forgive them.
Oscar Wilde, 1854–1900

Kids are like husbands – they're fine as long as they're someone else's
Marsha Warfield, 1954–

Given the pain involved in childbirth, perhaps it's no surprise that women feel put-upon by men. Anthropologists have suggested that men are scared of women's power to produce the next generation, and they react to that fear in the same way that they react to every other fear – they try to suppress the thing that causes the fear. Other anthropologists have suggested that men like football and gadgets because they are used, in an evolutionary sense, to throwing spears at things, while women gossip because, in the same way, they had to sit around a lot while they were pregnant. Sigmund Freud, the allegedly incestuous, paedophiliac junkie who founded psychotherapy, claimed that women are jealous of the fact that men have penises, although why men shouldn't be equally jealous of women's vaginas was never really explained – Freud's prejudices showing, perhaps? Whatever the reasons, though, the two sexes have traditionally spent about as much time being rude about each other as they have chasing after each other.

Men certainly get a lot of flak. Apparently, they're hairy, oversized, brutish, dumb, and they spend far too much time thinking about their favourite sports team. Malicious and cunning, they cruelly oppress women, cheat on them, lie, steal, and prove generally unreliable and ineffective. When you want a tolerable one, you won't be able to find one; later, when you're heartily sick of the lot of them, three will come along, just like buses.

One hell of an outlay for a very small return.
Glenda Jackson, 1937–, on men

A hard man's good to find – but you'll mostly find him asleep.
Mae West, 1892–1980

I feel sorry for men – they have more problems than women. In the first place, they have to compete with women as well as with each other.
Françoise Sagan, 1935–

I'd like to get to the point where I can be just as mediocre as a man.
Juanita Kreps, 1921–

Women want mediocre men, and men are working hard to become as mediocre as possible.
Margaret Mead, 1901–1978

They think they can act like God Almighty because they've got a cock and they can mend a flex.
Victoria Wood, on men

All men are rapists, and that's all they are. They rape us with their eyes, their laws, their codes.
Marilyn French, 1929–

What passes for woman's intuition is often nothing more than man's transparency.
George Jean Nathan, 1882–1958

Once a woman is made man's equal, she becomes his superior.
Margaret Thatcher, 1925–

You see an awful lot of smart guys with dumb women, but you hardly ever see a smart woman with a dumb guy.
Erica Jong, 1942–

Men are like car alarms. They both make a lot of noise no one listens to.
Diana Jordan, 1956–

Women, when they have made a sheep of a man, always tell him he's a lion.
Honoré de Balzac, 1799–1850

There are no great men, buster. There are only men.
Charles Schnee, 1891–1965

The more I see of men, the more I like dogs.
Madame de Stael, 1766–1817

Too often the strong, silent man is silent only because he does not know what to say, and is reputed strong only because he has remained silent.
Winston Churchill, 1874–1965

Probably the only place where a man can feel secure is in a maximum security prison, except for the imminent threat of release.
Germaine Greer

By comparison, if we are to listen to the bad press, women are vain, fickle, manipulative and evil-minded; they are impossible to comprehend. The originators of sin, they are impure and unclean. They talk too much, spend far too much money on clothes and are about as trustworthy as a rattlesnake – and as venomous. Although they can be visually attractive when young, they become every bit as repulsive when they get old.

All women become like their mothers. That is their tragedy. No man ever does. That is his.
Oscar Wilde, 1854–1900

There is one woman whom fate has destined for each of us. If we miss her, we are saved.
New York Times newspaper, 1948

Twenty million young women rose to their feet with the cry "We will not be dictated to!", and promptly became secretaries.
G.K. Chesterton, 1874–1936

Women are like elephants to me: I like to look at them, but I wouldn't want to own one.
W.C. Fields, 1879–1946

I look on the sex with something like the admiration with which I regard the starry sky on a frosty December night. I admire the beauty of the Creator's workmanship; I am charmed with the wild but graceful eccentricity of the motions; and I wish both of them goodnight.
Robert Burns, 1759–1796

Brigands demand your money or your life; women require both.
Samuel Butler, 1612–1680

To promote a woman to bear rule, superiority, dominion or empire above any realm, nation or city is repugnant to nature, contrary to God, a thing most contrarious to his revealed will and approved ordinance, and finally, it is the subversion of good order, of all equity and justice. For who can deny that it is repugnant to nature that the blind be appointed to lead and conduct those who see? That the weak, the sick, and impotent persons shall nourish and keep the whole and strong? And, finally, that the foolish, mad and frenetic shall govern the discrete, and give counsel to such as be of authority? For their sight in civil regiment is but blindness; their strength, weakness; their counsel, foolishness; and judgement, frenzy, if it be rightly considered...
John Knox, 1505–1572

It is only man, whose intellect is clouded by his sexual impulses, that could give the name of "the fair sex" to that undersized, narrow-shouldered, broad-hipped and short-legged race.
Artur Schopenauer, 1788–1860

Certain women should be struck regularly, like gongs.
Noël Coward, 1899–1973

Although the battle between the sexes seems likely to rage on for as long as there are folks on the planet, many people don't have any real objection to the opposite sex. They are without prejudice – they simply loathe everyone. People, it seems, are every bit as objectionable in general as they are in specific cases.

They are *only ten.*
Lord Northcliffe, 1865–1922, reminding his staff of the mental age of the readers of his newspapers.

I wish I loved the human race;
I wish I loved its silly face;
I wish I liked the way it walks;
I wish I liked the way it talks;
And when I'm introduced to one,
I wish I thought "what jolly fun".
Walter Raleigh, 1552–1618

Everywhere I go, I see people swirling about in a human cesspit of their own making.
Chief Constable James Anderton, 1932–

A man said to the Universe, "Sir, I exist."
"However," replied the Universe, "the fact has not created in me a

sense of obligation."
Stephen Crane, 1871–1900

The defect of equality is that we only desire it with our superiors.
Henri Bregne, 1837–1899

It is a sin to believe evil of others, but it is seldom a mistake.
H.L. Mencken, 1880–1956

If one looks with a cold eye at the mess mankind had made of his history, it is difficult to avoid the conclusion that he has been afflicted by some built-in mental disorder which drives him towards self-destruction. Murder within the species on an individual or collective scale is a phenomenon unknown in the whole animal kingdom, except for man, and a few varieties of ants and rats.
Arthur Koestler, 1905–1983

Mercy on us, that God should give his favourite children, men, mouths to speak with, discourse rationally, to promise smoothly, to flatter agreeably, to encourage warmly, to counsel wisely: to sing with, to drink with, and to kiss with: and that they should turn them into mouths of adders, bears, wolves, hyenas, and whistle like tempests, and emit breath through them like distillations of aspic poison, to asperse and vilify the innocent labour of their fellow creatures who are desirous to please them. God be pleased to make the breath stink and the teeth rot out of them all therefore!
Charles Lamb, 1775–1834

The common people are worth dying for until you bunch them together and give them a cold once-over, and then they impress the impartial observer as being slightly bovine, with a large percentage of vegetable tissue.
George Ade, 1886–1944

People – a group that in my view have always attracted an undue amount of attention – have often been likened to snowflakes. This analogy is meant to suggest that each is unique – no two are alike. This is quite patently not the case. People are quite simply a dime a dozen, and, I hasten to add, their only similarity to snowflakes resides in their invariable and lamentable tendency to turn, after a few warm days, to slush.
Fran Lebowitz, 1951–

All God's children are not beautiful. Most of God's children are, in fact, barely presentable.
Fran Lebowitz

The world, in its best state, is nothing more than a larger assembly of beings, combining to counterfeit happiness, which they do not feel, employing every art and contrivance to embellish life, and to hide their real condition from the eyes of one another.
Samuel Johnson, 1709–1784

The world is like a cucumber. Today it's in your hands, tomorrow it's up your ass.
Arab saying

It is the fools and knaves that make the wheels of the world turn. They are the world; those few who have sense or honesty sneak up and down single, but never go in herds.
George Saville, 1710–1784

The reason why fools and knaves thrive better in the world than wiser and honester men is because they are nearer to the general temper of mankind, which is nothing but a mixture of cheat and folly.
Samuel Butler, 1612–1680

Humanity, let us say, is like people packed in an automobile which is travelling downhill without lights at a terrific speed and driven by a small four-year-old child. The signposts along the way are all marked "Progress".
Lord Dunsany, 1878–1957

There is not a more mean, stupid, dastardly, pitiful, selfish, envious, ungrateful animal than the public. It is the greatest of cowards, for it is afraid of itself.
William Hazlitt, 1778–1830

We make the modern error of dignifying the individual. We do everything we can to butter him up. We give him a name, assure him that he has certain inalienable rights, educate him, let him pass on his name to his brats and when he dies we give him a special hole in the ground. But after all, he's only a seed, a bloom, and a withering stalk among pressing billions. Your individual is a pretty disgusting, vain, lewd little bastard. By God, he has only one right guaranteed to him in nature, and that is the right to die and stink to heaven.
Ross Lockridge, 1898–1962

The general average of mankind are not only moderate in intellect, but also moderate in inclinations; they have no taste or wishes strong enough to incline them to do anything unusual, and they consequently do not understand those who have, and class all such with the wild and intemperate upon whom they are accustomed to look down.
John Stuart Mill, 1806–1873

All men are born with a sufficiently violent liking for domination, wealth and pleasure, and with much taste for idleness; consequently all men want the money and the wives and daughters of others, to be their master, to subject them to all their caprices, and to do nothing, or at least to do only very agreeable things.
Voltaire, 1694–1778

It is always worth broadening your horizons. But there are far more things out there to be objectionable about than simply other humans and our relationships with them. Mankind's most basic need is for the fuel that keeps the body going. We spend a large portion of our lives buying, preparing and eating food. When done properly, food is one of the world's most sensual pleasures. How many of us have not, at one time or another, thought that perhaps a large bar of chocolate would be preferable to a relationship? When a meal turns out badly, though, it is a great and crushing disappointment, rather like a child who drops out of university to become a drug dealer. Well, maybe not quite like that, but the thought's certainly there in the following minds:

Surrounded with cold, white fat, the rabbit legs looked like maps of Greenland, and tasted like a dryad's inner thigh.
Clive James

Turkey is totally inedible. It's like eating a scrum half.
Willie Rushton, 1937–1996, on turkey

There is no dignity in the bean.
Charles Warner, 1829–1900

Cottage cheese – there's not flavour to it. It's like kissing your sister.
Anonymous

Gelée of duck had the consistency of Pamela Anderson Lee's implants, and was so salty and horrid it was like licking an Abyssinian shot-putter's armpit.
A.A. Gill, 1923–

A man of my spiritual intensities does not eat corpses.
George Bernard Shaw, 1856–1950, on meat

Dried fish is a staple food in Iceland – it varies in toughness. The tougher kind tastes like toe-nails, and the softer kind like the skin off the soles of one's feet.
W.H. Auden, 1907–1973

There is something sinister about anchovy, something insect-like and creepy, menacing, disturbing and fishily unfishy (unofficially).
Craig Brown, 1936–

Tofu. Girls, have you ever had a yeast infection? It's not two hundred miles away from what tofu looks like.
Ruby Wax, 1953–

Foods that are said to do one good generally taste of sawdust and burnt rubber.
R.H. Howarth, 1968–

The snails still had their horns and were curled up and wrinkled like frost-bitten snotty noses boiled to death in their beds.
A.A. Gill

I bit the head off a live bat the other night. It was like eating a Crunchie wrapped in chamois leather.
Ozzy Osborne, 1948–

The demon drink, alcohol, has attracted a lot of negative attention. For one thing, it makes people drunk. For another, even inferior booze costs so *much* these days...

Those who drink beer will think beer.
Washington Irving, 1783–1859

Drinking raw Absinthe is like swallowing a Bengal tiger.
Sylvia Townsend Warner, 1893–1964

I sipped the cognac. It tasted like semi-viscous airplane fuel from the Amelia Earhart era.
Kinky Friedman, 1944–, *When the Cat's Away*

Spanish wine, my God, it is foul – catpiss is champagne, compared – this is the sulphurous urination of some aged horse.
D.H. Lawrence, 1885–1930

Some of the most dreadful mischiefs that afflict mankind proceed from wine; it is the cause of disease, quarrels, sedition, idleness, aversion to labour, and every species of domestic disorder.
François de Salignac, 1651–1715

The metallic flavour of this particular claret gives it a slight prison flavour.
John Mortimer, 1923–

I wish to see beer become common instead of the whisky which kills one third of our citizens, and ruins their families.
Thomas Jefferson, 1743–1826

Drinks flowed like cement...
John Mortimer

God, what on earth was I drinking last night? My head feels like there's a Frenchman living in it.
Ben Elton, 1959–, and Richard Curtis, 1956–, *Blackadder II*

Normally, if your food and drink are unsatisfactory, you have only yourself or your nearest and dearest to blame. If you don't like the taste of boiled cabbage, for example, then do not buy, chop and boil cabbages. However, sometimes the quality of your victuals is totally outside your control. This is the case on those occasions where you put your sanity and your tastebuds on the line, and go to a restaurant.

Putting your name to this place would be on a par with Thomas Crapper naming a toilet after himself.
A.A. Gill, on The Hempel restaurant

Does anyone actually start the day with prunes, muesli, croissant and full English breakfast, except when they are visiting hotel-land? As for the "individual butter portions" the electron microscope which you would need to spread it is never supplied.
Victor Lewis-Smith, 1966–

Some of the waiters discuss the menu with you as if they were sharing wisdom picked up in the Himalayas.
Seymour Britchky, 1928–, *The Restaurants of New York*

I ordered the Corn Masa Blinis with Salsa Verde and Sour Cream... it looked as if someone had been sick over a passing plate. The taste, too, was not dissimilar.
Craig Brown, on Columbus restaurant, London

We ate baby vegetables so small it felt like infanticide.
Peter York, 1954–

Great restaurants are, of course, nothing but mouth-brothels.
Frederic Raphael, 1931–

Dog food is an overused amateur description for food and, in the general run of things, I'd steer clear of it, but this plate was so exactly precisely reminiscent of hot Chum that I can really do no better.
A.A. Gill

The food was as tastefully forgettable as... as... Oh, I can't remember.
A.A. Gill

Geographically, it is half-way between Elmer's End and Pratt's Bottom. Gastronomically, it is about the same.
Anonymous, about an unnamed restaurant in Bromley, Kent

Spud-U-Like – like the Department of Social Security, but with potatoes.
Victoria Wood

It is a silly place.
Lloyd Grossman, 1949–, on Le Gavroche restaurant, London, possibly citing Monty Python...

The 85 cent dinner tasted like a discarded mail bag and was served to me by a waiter who looked as if he would slug me for a quarter, cut my throat for six bits, and bury me at sea in a barrel of concrete for a dollar and a half plus sales tax.
Raymond Chandler, 1888–1959, *Farewell My Lovely*

Another favourite topic of conversation, particularly for men, is sport. You can stir up a lively little discussion by being rude about someone's favourite sport, so the following quotes are particularly useful for men, or for people who have to spend time in the vicinity of men. Which is, frankly, nearly everybody. Most of the various major sports available for lampooning are victimized below.

Have you seen him dance? Like God, he moves in mysterious ways.
Ann Winter, 1941–

He dances like a drunk killing cockroaches.
John Barbour, 1920–1995

Dancing with her was like moving a piano.
Ring Lardner, 1885–1933

I don't see the sense in American Football. I haven't since I became a vegetarian.
Dan Millman, 1945–

A bad soccer team is like an old bra – it has no cups and little support.
Anonymous, on soccer

I hate baseball. I have lots of reasons to hate baseball. For one it's dull. Nothing happens. Watching baseball is like going to a lecture by a member of the Slow... Talkers... Of... America. It's like turning on the TV when the cable is out. It's like watching grass – no, Astroturf – grow.
Jeff Jarvis, 1950–

The game is too long, the season is too long, and the players are too long.
Jack Dolph, 1886–1957, on basketball

The National Hockey League is so tightly organized that even the robber barons of old couldn't have devised a more monopolistic feudal system.
Nick Auf Der Maur, 1942–1998

A surfer is an American lemming.
Jacob Bronowski, 1904–1974

Joggers are basically neurotic, bony, smug types who could bore the paint off a DC-10. It is a scientifically proven fact that having to sit through a three-minute conversation between two joggers will cause your IQ to drop 13 points.
Rick Reilly, 1953–

If you are going to be getting some exercise, of course, nothing beats the countryside as a place to do it. I mean that literally. Nothing does, in fact, beat the countryside. Hands down.

I don't know which is the worst of the country, the walking or the sitting at home with nothing to do.
George Bernard Shaw, 1856–1950

I have no relish for the country; it is a kind of healthy grave.
Sydney Smith, 1771–1845

I was sat at the bottom of the garden a week ago, smoking a reflective cheroot, thinking about this and that – mostly that – and I just happened to glance at the night sky, and I marvelled at the millions of stars glistening like little pieces of quicksilver thrown carelessly onto black velvet. In awe, I watched the waxen moon ride across the zenith of the heavens like an amber chariot towards the void of infinite space wherein the tethered bolts of Jupiter and Mars hang forever festooned in all their orbital majesty, and as I looked at all this, I thought "I must put a roof on this bloody toilet."
Les Dawson, 1934–1993, on the great out-doors ... or is that the great out-house?

One of the great features of getting out of cities and into the countryside – apart from the smell of manure – is the sheer volume of animal life out there. The world is teeming with creatures of all shapes and sizes, and, according to several notables, all of them utterly repulsive. Others are more selective – just a sub-section of them are repulsive. As a side note, on the topic of revolting aspects of the animal kingdom, were you aware that if you weighed all the insects in the world on one big scale and all the humans in the world, the weight of the insects would be something like 10 times that of the humans? Now, there's five billion people or so, each one weighing as much as approximately 50,000 insects... Ugh.

I do not like animals, of any sort. I don't even like the idea of animals. Animals are no friend of mine. They are not welcome in my house. However, I like them just fine in the form of nice, crisp spare-ribs and Bass Weejun penny-loafers.
Fran Lebowitz, 1951–

It's a fine day. Let's go out and kill something.
Anonymous

Animals generally return the love you lavish on them by a swift bite in passing.
Gerald Durrell, 1925–1995

Dangerous at both ends, and uncomfortable in the middle.
Ian Fleming, 1908–1964, on horses

It's the one species I wouldn't mind seeing vanish from the face of the earth. I wish they were like the White Rhino – six of them left in the Serengeti National Park, and all males.
Alan Bennett, 1934–, on dogs

For many of us, particularly myself, a dog is a set of sharp teeth mounted on four legs.
Robert Morley, 1908–1992

Don't make the mistake of treating your dogs like humans, or they'll treat you like dogs.
Martha Scott, 1914–

Cat, n: A soft, indestructible automaton provided by nature to be kicked when things go wrong in the domestic circle.
Ambrose Bierce, 1842–1914, *The Devil's Dictionary*

God save all here, barring the cat.
Irish saying

No-one has ever actually called a cat ... they come when they wish.
Kinky Friedman, 1944–, *Elvis, Jesus and Coca-Cola*

The cat Percy, for all his sleek exterior, was mean and bitter. He had no music in his soul, and was fit for treasons, strategies and spoils. One could picture him stealing milk from a sick tabby.
P.G. Wodehouse, 1881–1975, *Cats Will Be Cats*

A camel looks like a horse that was planned by a committee.
Anonymous

The song of canaries never varies, And when they're molting, they're revolting.
Ogden Nash, 1902–1971, *The Canary*

The tortoise is the animal equivalent of a Tonka toy.
Nick Hancock, 1966–

If dolphins are so intelligent, how come they ain't got Walkmans?
John Lydon, 1956–

Dull, unmysterious city unemployables, dressed in their grey, second-hand suits.
Anthony Carson, 1949–, on pigeons

After animals, somehow the business community as a target seems to follow on naturally. Almost everyone hates working. That's why senior managers take such great pains to make sure they never actually have to do anything, and go and play golf together instead. In the pages that follow, you'll be taken on a whistlestop tour of the negative side of working life – the people. When you make it back to the office, there will be plenty of new negative things for you to say about the bulk of the people around you!

Don't get me wrong. I have nothing against businessmen. They are a necessary life form, like earthworms and dung beetles and the E. coli bacteria which inhabit the human gut. Without them we would have no shopping malls, junk mail, leisure complexes, direct insurance sales lines, dial-a-pizza services or countless other benefits of modern civilization.
John Naughton, 1940–

For every opportunity, they'll find a way to make some problems. For every success, they'll steal all your credit. For every failure, they'll deny their blame and pass it onto you. For every good idea, you can be sure they'll find someone to sack. No spite or incompetence is beneath them, no stupidity too obvious, no flattery too unsubtle, no vanity too tasteless. They are paid the majority of the money in the country in order to cause the majority of problems, which seems fair enough in a sick sort of way.
Tim Dedopulos, 1969–, on middle management

Show me a capitalist, and I'll show you a bloodsucker.
Malcolm X, 1926–1965

I find it rather easy to portray a businessman. Being bland, rather cruel and incompetent comes naturally to me.
John Cleese, 1939–, on businessmen.

I come from an environment where, if you see a snake, you kill it. At General Motors, if you see a snake, the first thing you do is hire a consultant on snakes. Then you spend a year talking about snakes.
Ross Perot, 1930–

Of all the trades, journalism probably gets the most amount of criticism. That might just be because many of them apparently tell the greatest number of libellous lies, about the greatest possible number of people, to everybody who is in range, in as loud a voice as they possibly can. On the other hand, it might be completely unrelated!

Once a newspaper touches a story, the facts are lost forever, even to the protagonists.
Norman Mailer, 1923–

America is a country of inventors, and the greatest inventors of all are the newspaper men.
Alexander Bell, 1847–1922

A foreign correspondent is someone who flies around from hotel to hotel and thinks that the most interesting thing about any story is the fact that he has arrived to cover it.
Tom Stoppard, 1935–, on journalists

The press can best be compared to haemorrhoids.
Gareth Davies, 1943–

I love the media. They should all be working from Dachau.
Jerry Lewis, 1926–

The enemy in question is that drivel-merchant, global huckster and so-to-speak media psychopath Rupert Murdoch, a Hannibal The Cannibal *who is in many important ways a deal more powerful in Britain than our own schoolboy Parliament, its minority-elected government, and even its bumbling Mr Pooter of a Prime Minister. A government – and God help us – that Mr Murdoch's press did so much, so dishonestly, to put into power, mostly by means so aslant, so tilted, so bent and untrue that they*

by definition open the trap-door under the word "democracy". If we cared two pence about our own culture, we ought to make sure that the next time Murdoch sets foot in this, his fiefdom, he should be arrested and put on public trial.
Dennis Potter, 1935–1996, on the media

The modern editor of a paper does not want facts. The editor wants novelty. He would prefer a novelty that is not a fact to a fact that is not a novelty.
William Randolph Hearst, 1863–1951

Journalism could be described as turning one's enemies into money.
Craig Brown, 1936–

It isn't just journalism that gets slated, though. The rest of the media are no better, according to some.

Most of the current literary and arts magazines are written by the self-indulgent or pretentious.
Rupert Vandervell, 1902–1987

There's no way anyone is going to take you seriously if you're on a TV show.
Shaun Cassidy, 1958–

Another lazy breed, like actors. These are likewise too lazy to read through their material before delivering it, and constantly misemphasize it, pause in the wrong place, etc.
Kingsley Amis, 1922–1995, on news readers

Radio is death in the afternoon, and well on into the night.
Arthur Miller, 1915–

The prospect of Dan Quayle running the world if George Bush drops dead is like having a radio DJ running the world.
John Peel, 1941–

Another group who everyone remembers with bitterness and hatred is teachers. We all had at least one cruel, incompetent, stupid teacher at school who stunted our intellectual development and left us with neuroses that lasted into adult life. Mine was called Mrs B– but no, there's no need to risk legal repercussions. Suffice it to say that these selfless maniacs have often gone unpunished and anonymous. Some people have taken a chance, in the past, to hit back.

The schoolteacher is certainly underpaid as a child-minder, but ludicrously overpaid as an educator.
John Osborne, 1929–

For all the smooth talk of modern headmasters, most English boarding schools were still hotbeds of racism and social prejudice.
A.N. Wilson, 1950–

I am inclined to think that one's education has been in vain if one fails to learn that most schoolmasters are idiots.
Hesketh Pearson, 1887–1968

Everybody who is incapable of learning has taken to teaching.
Oscar Wilde, 1854–1900

The most formidable headmaster I ever knew was a headmistress. She had X-ray pince-nez and that undivided bust popularized by Queen Mary. I think she was God in drag.
Nancy Banks-Smith, 1947–

Headmasters of private schools are divided into two classes – the workers and the runners-up-to-London.
P.G. Wodehouse, 1881–1975

God forgive me for having ever thought that a schoolmaster could be out and out a rational being.
Sir Walter Scott, 1771–1832

After teachers, there are of course bankers – a profession famous for the invisible "w" in their name.

He's called a broker because after you deal with him that's exactly what you are.
Anonymous

Accounting is a malicious extension of the banking conspiracy.
Henry Ford, 1863–1947

Accountants are the witch doctors of the modern world.
Mr Justice Harman, 1913–

He looked like an accountant or serial killer type. Definitely one of the service industries.
Kinky Friedman, *Elvis, Jesus and Coca-Cola*

An actuary is someone who moved out of accountancy because he couldn't stand the excitement.
Anonymous

Auditors are the troops who watch a battle from the safety of a hillside and when the battle is over, come down to count the dead and bayonet the wounded.
Anonymous

Consultants are people who borrow your watch to tell you the time and then walk off with it.
Robert Townsend, 1957–

You can make even a parrot into a learned political economist – all he must learn are the two words "Supply" and "Demand".
Anonymous

Economists are people who think that the poor need them to tell them that they are poor.
André Drucker, 1909–

There are plenty of other respectable professional groups who have also attracted a great deal of insults; police, priests, soldiers, lawyers... The material on lawyers alone could fill several libraries. Everyone hates lawyers, and with good reason. The choicest insults are *not* to be found below, though – I don't want to get sued!

First thing we do, let's kill all the lawyers.
Anonymous

Lawyers and painters can soon turn white to black.
Danish saying

Lawyers Can Seriously Damage Your Health
Michael Joseph, 1931–

A vague uneasiness – the police. It's like when you suddenly understand you have to undress in front of a doctor.
Ugo Betti, 1892–1953

The Metropolitan Police Force is abbreviated to the "Met" to give more of its

members a chance of spelling it.
Mike Barfield, 1961–

Librarians always look like librarians who are trying not to look like librarians. Even librarians who try not to look like librarians look like librarians trying not to look like librarians.
Anonymous

It's no accident that the symbol of a bishop is a crook, and the sign of an archbishop is a double-cross.
Dom Dix, 1891–1969

Operationally, God is beginning to resemble not a ruler but the last fading smile of a cosmic Cheshire cat.
Julian Huxley, 1887–1975

The professional military mind is by necessity an inferior and unimaginative mind; no man of high intellectual quality would willingly imprison his gifts in such a calling.
H.G.Wells, 1866–1946, on soldiers

There are three kinds of intelligence – the intelligence of man, the intelligence of animals, and the intelligence of the military. In that order.
Gottfried Reinhardt, 1873–1953

Scientists are supposed to be wise and open-minded, the shepherds of our knowledge and the guardians of our future. There are plenty of people, however, who seem quite convinced that they are all damn fools.

Verily, it is easier for a camel to pass through the eye of a needle than for a scientific man to pass through a door.
Sir Arthur Eddington, 1882–1944

An observatory is where astronomers conjecture away the guesses of their predecessors.
Ambrose Bierce, 1842–1914

Mathematics may be defined as that subject in which we never know what we are talking about, nor whether what we are saying is true.
Bertrand Russell, 1872–1970

First doctors try to get on, then they honour, then they get honest.
Humphrey Rolleston, 1865–1933

A dentist is a prestidigitator who, putting metal in your mouth, pulls coins out of your pocket.
Ambrose Bierce

Philosophers have always been happier in felling the orchards of their predecessors than in planting new ones.
Lambert Gefferies, 1910–1976

Forget about smacking children, when are we going to start hitting child psychologists?
Julie Burchill, 1959–

Psychiatrists have a financial interest in being wrong; the more children they can disturb, the larger their adult clientele.
Geoffrey Robertson, 1925–

I refuse to endure months of expensive humiliation only to be told that at the age of four I was in love with my rocking-horse.
Noël Coward, 1899–1973, on psychology

Hell hath no fury like a wallflower with a sociology degree.
Julie Burchill, on sociologists

One has to look out for engineers – they begin with sewing machines and end up with the atomic bomb.
Marcel Pagnol, 1895–1974

The end result of science, of course, is technology. This is normally defined as the physical equipment and techniques by which the world gets rapidly more confusing and unpleasant...

Sir, I have tested your machine. It adds a new terror to life and makes death a long-felt want.
Sir Herbert Beerbohm Tree, 1853–1917, on an early ancestor of the record player

The two big tricks of the twentieth century are technology instead of grace and information instead of virtue.
Ulysée Comtois, 1945–1990

If the human race wants to go to hell in a basket, technology can help it get there by jet. It won't change the desire or the direction, but it can greatly speed the passage.
Charles Allen, 1897–1969

We have genuflected before the god of science only to find that it has given us the atomic bomb, producing fears and anxieties that science can never mitigate.
Martin Luther King, 1929–1968

Science has taught us to kill before philosophy has taught us to think.
Lester Sinclair, 1878–1968

What's the average man's life but a succession of cars? When he dies, we should carve on his tombstone simply the makes and years.
Richard Needham, 1900–1995

It's like a 5.7 litre vibrator.
Jeremy Clarkson, 1960–, on the Lamborghini Diablo

The Chrysler Stratus looks like Pamela Anderson ... a silicone sham with no real depth.
Jeremy Clarkson

To buy a Volvo 540 because it is better than the Volvo 400 is like having someone to dinner because they are better company than Myra Hindley.
Jeremy Clarkson, not quite comparing a Volvo to a noted mass-murderess

This car is as enjoyable as muesli without the milk.
Tiff Needell, 1958–, on the Austin Metro

Having torn the world to shreds, it's time to return to that favourite topic of criticism – other people. The great and the good have had a lot to say that's frankly personal, and it's worth finishing up with a brief survey of some of the more amusing quotes. After all, there's so much to denigrate about people; their physical characteristics...

A laugh as jolly as an axe embedding itself in a skull.
William McIlvanney, 1936–, *The Kiln*

The speaking voice sounds like Rice Krispies would if they could talk.
John Simon, 1873–1954, on Barbra Streisand

I cannot bring myself to vote for a woman who has been voice-trained to speak

to me as though my dog has just died.
Keith Waterhouse, 1929–, on Margaret Thatcher

My pubic hair is a problem. It's all over the place, like some bloody rockery plant.
Victoria Wood, 1957–

A lady whose upswept hairstyle suggested that she had surfaced abruptly underneath a heron's nest.
Clive James

Hair like badly turned broccoli.
Clive James, on John McEnroe

Her hair lounges on her shoulders like an anaesthetized cocker spaniel.
Henry Allen, 1859–1930

You know Linford Christie? My genitals are like a sort of travel version of that.
Frank Skinner, 1965–; Linford Christie, a British athlete, is famed for his big penis

... and their appearance. People look strange, and some people look stranger than others.

He looked rather pleasantly like a blond Satan.
Dashiel Hammett, 1894–1961

I have always considered my face a convenience rather than an ornament.
Oliver Wendell Holmes, 1809–1894

My face looks like a wedding cake that has been left out in the rain.
W.H. Auden, 1907–1973

She was a really bad-looking girl. Facially, she resembled Louis Armstrong's voice.
Woody Allen, 1935–

I have eyes like those of a dead pig.
Marlon Brando, 1924–

His eyes look like a left-luggage office.
A.A. Gill, 1923–

He looked like a horse who, in addition to having a secret sorrow, had laryngitis as well.
P.G. Wodehouse, 1881–1975

He had a face like a collapsed lung.
Raymond Chandler, 1888–1959, *The Long Goodbye*

I guess I look like a rock quarry that has been dynamited.
Charles Bronson, 1922–

Once seen, that antique-mapped face is never forgotten – a bloodhound with a head cold, a man who is simultaneously biting on a bad lobster and caught by the neck in lift doors, a mad scientist's amalgam of Wallace Beer and Yogi Bear.
Alan Brien, 1925 –, on Walter Matthau

He looked as inconspicuous as a tarantula on a slice of angel cake.
Raymond Chandler

Descriptions of my face have included comparisons with most root vegetables.
Frankie Howerd, 1921–1992

She is a stern woman, who looks as if her idea of a good time would be knitting, preferably under the guillotine.
William McIlvanney, 1936–, *The Kiln*

Glenda Jackson has a face to launch a thousand dredgers.
Jack de Manio, 1912–1989, on Glenda Jackson

His nose peels in August like a Jersey potato.
Craig Raine, 1942–, *Misericords*

Her face looked like something on the menu in a seafood restaurant.
Woody Allen

He had a pair of buck teeth that made him look like the first cousin of a walrus.
Richard Brautigan, 1935–1994, *Dreaming of Babylon*

The body is another area where people can be quite peculiar. Of all the possible body areas to be critical of, it should come as no surprise that the most discussed – by women as well as men – is the female breast. Psychologists would no doubt talk about mother-fixation, suckling, the nurturing bosom, and all that sort of thing; women, who have far more experience in the matter, say simply that men are fairly obsessed with the damn things, and so they tend to worry about them too.

Demi Moore's breasts hang around Striptease *like a brace of silicon albatrosses.*
Mark Steyn, 1936–

Jogging bra-less by the canal, she looked like the original inspiration for Barnes Wallis.
Ann Winter, 1941–

Working with Sophia Loren is like being bombed with watermelons.
Alan Ladd, 1913–1964

How do you like them? Like a pear, a lemon, à la Montgolfier, half an apple, or a cantaloupe? Go on, choose, don't be embarrassed.
Colette, 1873–1954, on breasts

Nubs, stubs, eggs, cups, bloopers, droopers and Jesus!
Anon, on breasts

She had such big tits it looked like her arm was in a sling.
Alan Bennett, 1934–

Breasts came back after World War II – linked with dumb blondes in the most regrettable partnership since the sweet potato met the marshmallow.
Laura Shapiro, 1968–

How you dress has a huge effect on how people perceive you. Your clothing can emphasize or obscure aspects of your anatomy – although never as much as you'd like – and it makes comments about you as a person. Sometimes, those comments are rather insulting.

This lady, who had very black hair, had stuck over her right ear the pitiable corpse of a large white bird, which looked exactly as if someone had killed it by stamping on its breast, and then nailed it to the lady's temple – which was presumably of sufficient solidity to bear the operation.
George Bernard Shaw, 1856–1950

In a sweater, she looked like a walking dairy state.
Joan Rivers, 1933–

Tell me the history of that frock, Judy. It's obviously an old favourite. You were

wise to remove the curtain rings.
Barry Humphries ("Dame Edna Everage"), 1934–, to Judy Steel

She was always wearing a loose bathrobe that covered up a body that would have won first prize in a beauty contest for cement blocks.
Richard Brautigan, *Dreaming of Babylon*

Have you ever seen how he dresses to jog? He wears what looks like a pair of Babe Ruth's old swimming trunks and a PE-issue plain grey T-shirt. I mean, I still believe in a place called Hope – unless it's where he shops for jogging clothes.
Rick Reilly, 1953–, on Bill Clinton

I don't own a dress. I wear skirts, but I look like a netball teacher.
Victoria Wood

A monastic monstrosity in baggy rags and combat boots – a creepy cross between Joan of Arc and Kojak.
Anonymous, on Sinead O'Connor

Some people are born with a sense of how to clothe themselves, others acquire it, others look as if their clothes had been thrust upon them.
Saki, 1870–1916

Today's Hollywood stars – even the real lookers like Michelle Pfeiffer and Winona Ryder – are shy, troubled creatures who dress like something Cat Stevens dragged in from the local Saturday-night sackcloth-and-ashes hop.
Julie Burchill, 1959–

Compared to him, an audience of AC/DC heavy-metal fans would win prizes for couture.
The Observer newspaper, 1992–, on fashion designer Alexander McQueen

There is something wrong – even histrionic – about a man who wears white spats with a black shirt.
Ernest Hemingway, 1898–1961, on Benito Mussolini

There are few targets as obvious for a handy put-down as offensive body odour. Hygiene is an important part of daily life in an environment where people are crammed in together. It only takes one sweaty commuter to turn the stomachs of an entire carriage-load of people. Some people are supposed to be totally unable to smell human body odour – presumably they're the ones who stink, so if that could be corrected, the world might be a far more pleasant place.

It may be December outside, ladies, but under your armpits it is always August.
John Snagge, 1904–1980

He smelled as if he had just eaten a mustard-coated camel.
Martin Amis, 1949–, *London Fields*

W.G. Grace had one of the dirtiest necks I have ever kept wicket behind.
George Cobham, 1819–1863

I don't understand anything about ballet. All I know is that during the intervals the ballerinas stink like horses.
Anton Chekov, 1860–1904

You smell like the toasted cheese sandwiches my mother used to bring me.
Anthony Perkins, in *Psycho II*

Bathe twice a day to be really clean, once a day to be passably clean, and once a week to avoid being a public nuisance.
Anthony Burgess, 1917–

Henry IV's feet and armpits enjoyed an international reputation.
Aldous Huxley, 1894–1963

Life has the last laugh on all of us, though. From the moment we are born, we are getting older. Ageing is the beginning of the end – for people in general, for you yourself, and for this book, too.

Being a balding forty-something chap with bad teeth and a young, pretty girlfriend is the social equivalent of wearing a chest wig, a medallion, dyeing your hair and driving an E-type Jaguar with Barry White full blast on the stereo.
A.A. Gill

There are three classes of elderly woman – first, that dear old soul; second, that old woman; third, that old witch.
Samuel Taylor Coleridge, 1772–1834

Growing old is more like a bad habit which a busy man has no time to form.
André Maurois, 1885–1967

I'm ageing about as well as a beach-party movie.
Harvey Fierstein, 1954–

Growing old is like being increasingly penalized for a crime you haven't committed.
Anthony Powell, 1905–

She is a lady of a "certain age", which means she is certainly aged.
Lord Byron, 1788 –1824

I look like Barbara Cartland without the vitamins.
Victoria Wood

You are not permitted to kill a woman who has injured you, but nothing forbids you from reflecting that she is growing older every minute.
Ambrose Bierce, 1842–1914

I need another birthday like a hole in the head.
Dorothy Parker, 1893–1967

The years that a woman subtracts from her age are not lost. They are added to the ages of other women.
Diane de Poitiers, 1499–1566

Experience is a good teacher, but her fees are very high.
W.R. Inge, 1860–1954

If you want to know how old a woman is, ask her sister-in-law.
Edward Howe, 1853–1937

I prefer old age to the alternative.
Maurice Chevalier, 1888–1972